Living in Freedom & Love Without Conditions

New Paradigm Multi-Dimensional Transformation™

PHYLLIS M. BROOKS

BALBOA.
PRESS
A DIVISION OF HAY HOUSE

Cover illustration from a silk painting "I Merge With My Soul" by Phyllis Brooks

Balboa Press books may be ordered through booksellers or by contacting:

Balboa Press
A Division of Hay House
1663 Liberty Drive
Bloomington, IN 47403
www.balboapress.com
1 (877) 407-4847

Because of the dynamic nature of the Internet, any web addresses or links contained in this book may have changed since publication and may no longer be valid. The views expressed in this work are solely those of the author and do not necessarily reflect the views of the publisher, and the publisher hereby disclaims any responsibility for them.

The author of this book does not dispense medical advice or prescribe the use of any technique as a form of treatment for physical, emotional, or medical problems without the advice of a physician, either directly or indirectly. The intent of the author is only to offer information of a general nature to help you in your quest for emotional and spiritual well-being. In the event you use any of the information in this book for yourself, which is your constitutional right, the author and the publisher assume no responsibility for your actions.

Print information available on the last page.

ISBN: 978-1-5043-2755-8 (sc)
ISBN: 978-1-5043-2757-2 (hc)
ISBN: 978-1-5043-2756-5 (e)

Library of Congress Control Number: 2015902003

Balboa Press rev. date: 02/24/2015

Dedicated to John Armitage, Master Germain and
the other Multi-dimensional Masters who are making
themselves available to help humanity discover who we
really are during this time of dimensional transition.

CONTENTS

MULTI-DIMENSIONAL MASTER GERMAIN

During the last days of Atlantis, I was the leader of a group called the Inspirers. We decided it was time to leave the island we had been living on for years. The island was called Undaal, in the area that you know now as the Mediterranean Sea. We knew there was going to be another round of earth changes and did not want to be on the island when it happened.

We went off and looked for a better place for us to live. We arrived in the land you now know as Tibet. We met there a number of people you may now call holy men or monks. After we had been with them for awhile, I decided to give them a number of symbols and some information on how to use them. Then we waited until they had used it for a bit, to see how they got on. Maybe they would use it the same way as I had intended when I incarnated the system, to empower people. This was the idea behind it. We won't give you another history lesson, except to tell you there was a lot of control going on at the time. The caste system that still lives in India had been created, and many people were oppressed, because they were considered to be inferior to the controllers (in Atlantis). Most were even controlled by crystals that were implanted in the base of the brain. Sound familiar? Remember the plans to microchip the planet now! Anyway, they were denied access to all knowledge that would free them: knowledge of the true nature of the Self, the LOVE they truly were, and the freedom they deserved.

Some of the symbols were lost, some were contorted and used for control, and some were kept safe and only used by a few. The rest is history. Enter our friend Dr. Usui, on the search for freedom, and he found some of the symbols. How does not matter, really, the point is that he found a few of them, and he used them, adding a few Buddhist symbols to round out the system, and the system that is known as Usui Reiki was born. He passed it on to a number of people, and they helped to spread it around.

He never said, "You have to do this thing, that thing, and use this symbol" and so on. This was all brought into being later by the people who brought it to America. The original master in America even gave everybody different versions of the symbols to use. After her death, the 22 or so masters she had taught found this out by comparing the symbols they had been given. Except for the master symbol, which by the way is not correct anyway. Why? Because it is Japanese Kanji, and that form of writing was not around in Atlantean times. The energy behind the original Atlantean symbols grows and develops with humanity; that which the Kanji symbols represents does not.

So New Paradigm Multi-Dimensional Transformation is a reincarnation of my original project in Atlantis, to bring freedom to the earth and the people, with true knowledge of LOVE and self empowerment, knowledge of the self and the I AM, and our connection with all creation. It is, as some have pointed out, a great way to gain enlightenment and your personal ascension. In the meantime, you can facilitate healing for others and help them to enlightenment as well, and you can heal yourself and send loving energy to Mother Earth.

You will never save anybody or the earth, because nobody needs saving. All are on their path, and it's all personal choice.

God bless you and keep you all! Shamballa On!

Ascended Master Germain, channeled by John Armitage/Hari Das Baba

John Armitage

JOHN ARMITAGE, AKA HARI DAS BABA

I AM Love, I AM Light, I AM the Mahatma! I came to earth to help to ground LOVE and LIGHT. This mission has taken me on a journey of discovery, with humans, angels, archangels, the ascended masters, the galactic masters, and many other beings from other star systems and multi-dimensional realities. I have not had many lives on this beautiful planet, the goddess Gaia; this is my 123rd.

I was here first before Lemurian times, then during Lemuria. What a time we had, meditating the blueprints of crystalline forms into reality! Quartz, rosy quartz, aquamarine, tourmaline, amethyst, and roses were a few I helped to ground into 3rd dimension. I also helped to set up the earth energy grid and install and program the earth keeper crystals. I was also here in Atlantean times. They were interesting days, very much as things are now: many people into Love and Light, crystals and natural remedies, and many ones into the energy of war, control, fear and oppression.

After that I have had many lives in India, Tibet, Burma and Nepal, with the odd life here and there in between. I was with Shah Jehan at Agra, with Francis at Assisi, with Kuthumi in Kashmir, with Djwhal Khul in Tibet, with Wotanna in New Mexico, and with Sananda in Palestine.

Many of us have worked over many lifetimes to bring love to the earth and her people.

Massive changes are happening. We can become LOVE with grace and elegance. Why wait? Do it now. I AM now working on the next phase of the activation of the earth's grids. Of course, I AM not doing this alone—lots of people are playing their part in the plan, often not knowing that they are part of a worldwide plan to open pathways for the new energies—energies of Mahatma to flow and thus speed everybody's journey to freedom.

Keep up the good work, bless you all, Hari Das Baba.

AUTHOR'S INTRODUCTION

Traveling across the country with practically nothing left in my bank account seems like a leap of faith, but when I took off for Mt. Shasta, CA in September of 1998 I didn't think of it like that. I felt that at last I was grabbing on to my destiny. I didn't put it into so many words, or even concepts at the time, but I knew that I had to go to this workshop. There was no question at all about that. I'd known since April, when I first heard about it and met John Armitage. This was where I was supposed to be.

The venue presented a daunting juxtaposition of contrasts. We were in a beautiful 10-sided space with views of Mt. Shasta. Across the street in one of the other directions was a white church. Across to the other side was a church painted black, even the windows. I now feel that this was an omen that we would need to exercise discernment at all times.

The 27 participants were a strange mixture from many lands. How did they all find out about this class, and what drew them? I assumed they had been called as I had, that they had listened to that small voice inside that said, "GO!" This was true for at least some, and they became my friends.

The facilitators were also a strange duo. They didn't seem to get along very well, which wasn't surprising since they seemed to be exact opposites in many ways. John, the one I had come to learn from, was an Englishman. He could channel other dimensional beings as easily as have a conversation. He wasn't egotistical about this, just matter of fact. He told us some amazing and sometimes frightening things about our world, but always I felt he spoke truth. He believed with his whole self in freedom, and he told us not to give our power away to anyone, even him. The other facilitator was bombastic, egotistical, and controlling. I later found out power was the main thing he was after, as much as possible from as many as possible.

So the week was one of contrasts. We listened, went on amazing etheric journeys and had adventures with the beings from Telos, Australian medicine people, our own higher Selves, and others. We hung out in the copper-tube stargate built in the center of the room. We released, released, and released some more—at least those who were willing to release. John told us that energy moved when we told it to, and we began to believe him. We changed. Master Germain warned us at the end that we could not expect to go back and just take up our lives where we had left off. One man had a dream before he left home that he wasn't going to return; he was afraid this meant he was going to die during the journey. He realized by the end of the workshop that he was not the same as when he had come, so the old "he" was NOT returning. The 9 days was a rebirth of sorts, a birthing into our true Selves.

Germain also revealed on the last day that we had been on Galactic TV, so to speak. Beings from all over the universe were watching us. We were experimental guinea pigs. They were watching to see what would help humanity to grow rapidly, to raise their frequency to the levels necessary for ascension. I laughed at finding this out. The old me might have been upset at such surveillance, but the new me was delighted to be of service, and filled with joy and light.

The feeling of euphoria lasted about two weeks when I got home, but the changes continued, and do continue to the present. Master Germain,

John Armitage/Hari Baba, and all of the "Upstairs Department" as he calls them, have taken us, through the subsequent years, on a fantastic journey into ourselves. I would not have missed it for the world. And yes, I believe that I was destined for this journey, that I signed up for it before coming in this time around. I feel blessed to be a part of the New Paradigm MDT continuing program to connect humans to the truth about themselves and their place in the universe. This is an amazing time to be alive. We can ride the wave in joyful exuberance, or we can splash around fighting the current (and most of us do both from time to time). But I have found riding the wave of change to be my goal and my destiny. Baba and Germain woke me up. I refuse to sleep my way through this experience, this wonderful opportunity. I hope that this book will help to open readers to the realities and possibilities of being human at this time, and that they too will want to joyfully jump on the wave and ride it into our unimaginable future.

NOTE ON CHANNELED MATERIAL

Messages in this book from the multi-dimensional Master Germain and other beings not in physical body at this time are as they were channeled through John Armitage (hereafter J.A.), and they are usually in italics (unless otherwise indicated). John's own words are marked as such (J.A.).

"Channeling" is merely a means of communication between entities of different worlds and dimensions. The "channel" is the tube of light, or antahkarana, which connects the major chakras in the body to each other, as well as grounding them into the earth, and connecting upwards (in frequency) through the cosmic aspects of our being, to Source (depending on the vibrational rate of the channeler). Baba tells us that channeling is a natural talent, usually suppressed nowadays, but intrinsic to the human makeup. No channeling is 100% accurate at this time, as the message is being translated through the psyche of the channeler and is inevitably colored by his or her emotional body. 50-60% accuracy is considered *very* good. Germain has told John that his accuracy is above 85%.

Trance channeling is always correct, not necessarily the information contained in the channeling, but the words of the entity being channeled are exactly what they are saying; of course, the entity can be a trickster. John does not do or advocate trance channeling, because he does not give his body away completely to another entity. As he often says, "Don't give your power away to anybody or anything!" See the section on channeling for more information.

CHAPTER 1

WHAT IS *NEW PARADIGM MULTI-DIMENSIONAL TRANSFORMATION* AND WHERE DOES IT COME FROM?

THE ENERGY OF SHAMBALLA GROUNDED IN 3D

In a late Atlantean lifetime, Multi-dimensional Master Germain (often known as St. Germain, a family name in one of his other lifetimes) brought to earth a healing system. The purpose of this system was to help to raise the vibrational level of beings who had been created (by some of the Atlantean scientists) to be used as slaves. He and his group, the Inspirers, intended to help them to freedom. The system comprised 20 energies, held in 20 symbols.

When the group realized that the days of Atlantis were numbered, they left their home on one of the remaining islands. In their travels they came to what is now known as Tibet. There they encountered priest-types who were interested in learning the healing system. Germain gave them a few symbols to see how they would use them. When he saw that they were creating a secret system which gave them power over others, he decided they were not yet ready for the whole system and gave them no more symbols.

In the early 1900's, a Japanese Buddhist monk discovered these few symbols in Sanskrit scriptures he was studying. His name was Dr. Usui. He realized that the system was not complete, so he added a few Kanji Buddhist symbols and created what is now known as Reiki.

By the late 1980's Germain was not enthusiastic about the systems of control that had grown up around Reiki. Also, humans were now ready for much higher energies than they were in Dr. Usui's lifetime. He wanted to bring to earth the full system—not just the energies of the 20 symbols of the Atlantean system, but the whole spectrum of energies, 352 of them, one for each dimensional level back to Source. He planned to do this in steps, first extending the Reiki system and then quickly moving on, bringing in higher and higher frequencies.

This was envisioned to help humans wake up to their true identity, by connecting with the higher vibrational parts of themselves. Then they could begin to live in freedom—freedom from fear, freedom from the illusion of victimhood, freedom to live their potential according to the Divine Plan. The earth was beginning her ascension process, and if humans wanted to go along with her, they needed to release all their old programming of being sinners, victims, less-than. They needed to awaken to their divinity and allow Love without condition to flow through their being. They needed to stop judging themselves and others, and live in freedom.

He approached a friend of his, Dr. John Armitage, to spearhead this campaign of awakening people. John was not enthusiastic about anything to do with Reiki. To him it had become a system of control that charged people thousands to learn something intrinsic to them. It was another multi-dimensional friend of his who was able to convince him to take on the project. Kuthumi told John, "At this stage, what the energy of Shamballa is about is connecting people with their I Am

Presence, getting people to find out who and what they really are, allowing people to connect to their guidance."

Originally Master Germain named the system after the collective consciousness of the multi-dimensional Masters, Shamballa, through which these energies come to us from Source. Due to a lawsuit in 2012 we had to change our name. We still work with the energies of Shamballa, also known as the Great White Brotherhood or Brotherhood of Light ("white" here, of course, referring to the color of Light when all frequencies are present, not some ignorant idea of skin color or race. All of the people here on earth are of the Human race).

Our new name better represents who and what we really are. Master Germain regretted using the term "healing" in the original name. Nobody can heal anyone but his or her own Self. People can become healing facilitators, but the actual healing is up to the person involved. The focus of Germain's system, whatever it is called, is to awaken humans to their own divinity, to help free themselves from fear, and to open their hearts to Love without condition, without judgement. So we still use the energies of Shamballa, we just have renamed our school and organization.

Originally Germain had decided to make use of the advertising that had made "Reiki" a household word. "It was my system to begin with, so we might as well make use of it," he told John. "Soon we'll drop the name Reiki altogether." So when John started teaching in the mid-1990's, Reiki was part of the title. Germain gave John a few more of the original symbols, but he also had him activating his students to all 352 symbols, or energies, of the complete system, one for every level back to Source.

By 1998 he told us to drop the term Reiki. The system's energy had quickly moved way beyond Reiki, which was the original plan.

Germain later regretted bringing it in under the Reiki banner to begin with. He has said, "Of course I am not always perfect in the way I understand the human thought processes. I never dreamed that humans would have so much trouble in letting go and moving on. I didn't think that many would not feel able to free themselves from the old conditioning and stand in their own power. I really can't understand that, for remember that the nature of creation is forward movement, and that continues forever and ever." His remedy was to require more classroom hours, in order to give people more time with the multi-dimensional Masters, to help them through their resistance; and also a more rigorous program to train teachers. This new system went into effect during 2004-2007.

New Paradigm Multi-Dimensional Transformation is a continually expanding program of personal growth. The workshops are experiential, designed to move energy. We discuss concepts and explain about our multi-dimensional bodies, chakras, light bodies, DNA, etc., but we also experience guided meditations which help us to clear out old low frequency energies that we have held on to for lifetimes. The workshops are designed to help people move through their fears into the state of being of Love without conditions, without judgment. We are given the opportunity to integrate the highest frequency light energies available on the planet, to the extent each is able under the guidance of their own I Am Presence, or Higher Self, and activate ascension codes long-buried within our multi-dimensional structure. We learn how we are the architects of our own experiences here on earth, and if we don't like what we are experiencing, we can change it (by changing our attitudes, thoughts and actions).

At the core of these teachings is the state-of-being of Love without conditions. From experiencing this state comes connection with our higher Selves (our I Am Presence and higher frequency multi-dimensional and cosmic aspects), knowledge of who we really are, freedom and joy. We learn that the path of mastery is just that, a path; and that true mastery is nothing more, and nothing less, than mastery of the Self.

WHAT DO THESE TERMS MEAN?

At this time, the whole earth and humanity are making a multi-dimensional shift from 3D through 4D to 5D and higher. Our physical bodies and light bodies are TRANSFORMING, in order to be able to hold more light, higher frequencies. The shift and the vibrational increase are both caused by and are causing PARADIGM shifts throughout the world—different ways of seeing and understanding. We are undergoing a crystalline TRANSFORMATION, a frequency TRANSFORMATION, a PARADIGM-shift TRANSFORMATION. We are part of a process that is ongoing at this time, cause and effect intertwined, from our point of view. And our point of view is expanding MULTI-DIMENSIONALLY.

WHAT IS *SHAMBALLA*—Master Germain through J.A.

Shamballa is a place in time and space, or Shamballa is a number of places in time and space. When I say a number of places in time and space, I mean that in every dimensional reality there exists Shamballa. So what really is Shamballa? In some ways I see the easiest way of explaining this to you is that Shamballa is a place in time and space where harmony, balance and love is the totality of the energy. If you wanted to see Shamballa in your mind, or in your mind's eye, you can see Shamballa as a crystalline city of light. This is what you are connected with when you receive activations to the New Paradigm MDT energies, the Shamballa energies.

So where does the closest aspect of Shamballa exist? The closest aspect of Shamballa to your dimensional reality exists in the fifth dimension. But at this time, as the vibrations of the planet heighten or rise, sometimes there is an intermingling of the fifth dimension with the third or fourth dimension. This brings about sometimes very interesting results. Shamballa starts to manifest upon your planet as a city of light. So where does it manifest? If you could think about a map of your world in your dimensional reality, that area which takes in Mongolia, the place that is known as the Mongolian steps. This also, as well, spreads south towards the country of Tibet on top of the Himalayas. This is where the energy of Shamballa anchors into your dimensional reality.

It is also interesting to note that during these times, when the vibrations are so high upon the planet and Shamballa starts to manifest into your dimensional reality, that some of the governments of the world see Shamballa manifest. Shamballa is perceived by them by means of the satellites that they have flying around the earth. Some of these satellites have very powerful imaging devices, and all of a sudden they see upon their screens something new that wasn't there before. So they start to zoom in on this manifestation. You should realize that these satellites are powerful enough to zoom in on you to see which page of which newspaper you are reading in your garden. So when they see Shamballa manifesting, it makes them think a lot. They send their airplanes to check it out. Usually by the time the airplanes get there, Shamballa has again disappeared.

So that is the first manifestation of Shamballa, from the fifth dimension. But you, my friends, the New Paradigm MDT family of *light that live around the whole of this world, are the means by which Shamballa continually manifests itself energetically into your dimensional reality. As you focus, or as you keep yourselves aware of the fact that you can continuously bring through or ground the energy of Shamballa, through the New Paradigm MDT™, you can hold connections with multi-dimensional Shamballa.*

Master Germain has also told us that the grounding of New Paradigm MDT on the planet at this time represents a bringing together of the Violet Tribe. Master Germain is Chohan of the Seventh Ray, the Violet Ray of Transmutation. People come into each lifetime under the vibration of a certain Ray, according to who they are and what they wish to accomplish during that lifetime. You don't have to be of the Violet Ray in order be activated to the NPMDT/Shamballa energies, but many who find themselves called to a NPMDT class have incarnated this lifetime under this Ray.

THE FOUNDER IN 3D, JOHN ARMITAGE, aka Hari Das Baba

John was born in England in 1945, moving early on with his family to Ireland. Being the prototype for the later so-called "Indigo" children, he had a lot of trouble in school. His brain was not set up to learn in conventional ways, and his spirit rebelled at the constriction of formal education. He also had a stammer that made public speaking difficult. He was familiar with multi-dimensional beings and spoke with them from a very early age, however. He also spent 3 ½ years in India during his teens, studying to be a Brahmin. His guru once told John that John had been HIS guru in the last lifetime, and that the ashram they were staying in at the time was actually John's temple! So here, in his own words, is how John developed into the founder of New Paradigm Multi-Dimensional Transformation™.

When I was young, I never actually spoke until I was around 7 years old. My sister used to do all the talking for me. She always knew what I wanted. When she got older and grew fed up with it, my younger sister took over. After awhile she got fed up, too, so I had to speak for myself. When I had to speak for myself, I realized I couldn't speak, anyway, not in any proper way. I couldn't speak one word without stammering, seriously, seriously stammering. The first time I learned to speak without stammering was when I learned the sacred language, Hebrew. When I was living in Israel, I found that I could speak Hebrew without stammering. As soon as I had to speak English, I'd stammer all over again, on every word. Also, as well, when I was in school I couldn't read or write. So later on I taught myself to read, because I thought that would be a useful thing. I worked on teaching myself to read. In fact, I'm still learning to write, as anyone who takes an email off of me will understand. Really, in many ways, I am still learning to write.

As the years went on, and I did more and more traveling, more and more so-called spiritual things, I spent time in countries where people didn't speak my language. That meant that I didn't have to speak to anybody. I didn't speak their language, they didn't speak mine. Perfect, we'll all just hang out.

When I was around 28, I started to get guidance. I must say, I've had guidance ever since I was a small baby. I've known about the angels, and Masters, and everything else, and I'd been healing with my hands, and all the rest of it. But when I was around 28, I started to get guidance on how to control stammering. I still stammer now and then, but I've learned how to control it. What I do is, if I ever sit there and I'm going uh, uh, uh, then you know that I've shut my brain down temporarily, so that everything goes into neutral; everything will just catch back together again, and then I can continue. That's how I learned how to do it. So when I was about 28, I started to integrate how to start to control the stammer. Then it came time for my first experiences in public life, which meant I had to speak. When I was in my late teens, living in India with a bunch of Sadhus, often they'd give philosophical discourse, worship deities, whatever; my thing was to give people healing. That's how I earned my rice every day. Sometimes we'd go to places, and 3 or 4 or even 5 hundred people would come. I never had to say anything. So then came this time I knew I would have to speak publicly. I didn't quite know how that would manifest.

I always knew, from when I was a small child, that by doing some kind of thing or other I would help people to make changes in their lives. But I didn't know what it was. I was brought up as a Christian. My father was a preacher. In my early teens I used to wonder how I would get on at the college where I would study to be a minister, and how I would serve, with that stammer. I mean I used to think I would be a bishop or something.

One day I was walking along the street in a town called Weston-sur-Mer, a Victorian seaside town. I saw this sign, "First National Spiritualist Church." I thought, "That's interesting," and Chang (my major guide since childhood, who I later found out is really Lao Tzu) says to me, "Why don't you go in there?" "Yeah, alright." So I walked in, and there were people sitting there, with a platform up front. I sat down in the back. No one noticed when I walked in. I had hair down to below my shoulders, frizzed out, bell-bottom jeans, and everything. There was a lady up there who said she was going to demonstrate the continuity of life. She was going to do some clairvoyance. Immediately she opened her eyes and looked at me and said, "YOU!" I wondered, "What's going on here?" She said, "You, aren't you going to acknowledge me?" I said, "Yeah, OK."

So then she started telling me, in front of the whole church, some of the things that were going to happen to me in the future. Also as well, about some of my family. One of my grandfathers was actually what I would call a grass-roots herbalist; he was also into healing, in his own way. She said he was hanging around me. Afterwards I was trying to get out of the door; by then I was totally anti-church and all that kind of thing, with the exposure I'd had as a youngster. An elderly lady came up and said, "Nice to see you. I've actually been waiting three Sundays for you to arrive. We always have tea and biscuits afterwards. Would you like to have some tea?" So I did.

She invited me to join a special group they had. It soon became clear that the reason I'd been brought into the church was to go through some kind of training. I was assigned to this elderly lady as a pupil. She became my guru for a time. She was in her 60's. What she told me was that I'd been chosen by the Masters to bring messages to the people of Earth. She reinforced a lot of things I'd known since I was a small boy, but I still didn't see how I was going to do it, because every time I opened my mouth I stuttered. She said, "That doesn't matter. We can get around that."

So there I was, within a couple of classes, channeling. She said I was ready for my first public channeling. I told her I could give a good sermon (my mother writes great sermons, and I thought I could ask her to write a sermon for me). But I said, "Who's going to take care of the clairvoyance?" She said, "It's alright, love, I'll take care of it." So I turned up the next Sunday and found myself on the platform. I gave my sermon without stammering too much. I asked her who was going to do the clairvoyance, and she said, "You are." I said, "You said you'd take care of it!" And she said, "I have."

So me, I'm freaked out. I'd smoked a few spliffs, just to get me through it, but they didn't seem to make any difference. I still felt freaked out. I thought, "Shit, I'm not going to be able to do this, I'm not going to be able to do this!" So I thought I'd just get up and say I couldn't do it. I stood up, and was about to open my mouth and say, "Sorry about this," when I looked out and saw all these etheric beings. "This is really cool," I thought. "That must have been some good stuff!" Just joking. Then Chang said to me, "OK, boy, let's go for it! Just open your mouth."

So I opened my mouth, and I couldn't stop for about a half hour. What I realized was, if I surrendered to the process, then it was easy. After that I found myself, for the next 2 years, every Sunday, in a different part of England, on the circuit. Then I worked out that I could channel my sermons as well, and that it was dead easy to do.

After a few years, I realized it wasn't taking me anywhere, and that wasn't what I wanted to do. I found the philosophy very restrictive. My guru, God bless her, she only had knowledge from book 2½ or so, and I was looking for knowledge from book 5 or 10. When I'd ask her about something she didn't have any experience of, or couldn't tune in on, she'd tell me it "wasn't relevant" and "don't do it". I was getting information from other places saying, "come on Das, work on this." I'd also been facilitating a lot of healing, and I used to get a lot of information when I was doing this. Then I decided to stop public channeling.

As the years went by, I was doing research on crystals, homeopathy, and all. I channeled a thesis on homeopathy from Chang [Lao Tzu, author of the *Tao Te Ching*]. That's the way you get degrees. Me, I know nothing about homeopathy, and I've got a bachelor's degree. I don't need to know anything, because I know a man who does! So I was working with all of that stuff, a bit of channeling Ashtar in small groups, but I never thought I'd channel to large groups.

One day Sananda came to me. "Right, then, I'm going to be the next one you're working with," he told me. I said, "I'm not sure I'm ready to channel you, Jesus." And he said, "How long are you going to keep insisting you can't do it? How long are you going to go on reinforcing the block?" So I said, "Give me something I can work with to help resolve this block." He said, "OK, every night before you go to sleep, affirm, 'Sananda, I am worthy of channeling you.'" He said, "I already know that you're worthy of channeling me, so you're not trying to convince me. You've got to convince your subconscious mind that you're worthy. One of these days, I'm going to come and knock on your door, and you'll just open your mouth, and everything will work." So that's what I did for the next month or so. Every night before I went to bed I said, "Sananda, I am worthy of channeling you." I just tell you this story to share with you something of my own path of channeling. When I tell you these things, I don't see myself as a teacher, I see myself as a person who can share his life experiences with others, experiences that MIGHT, just MIGHT give them the inspiration to go forward. Just get over the judgment you have of yourselves. If you have these blockages somewhere deep in your psyche that you're not worthy of channeling the Masters or whoever, just start making the affirmations that you ARE.

Here in the New Paradigm MDT™ family some say to me, "Well Baba, we only work with a limited number of Multi-dimensional Masters." In fact, we don't work with a limited number of them. But for ease, we just name a few of them. People become familiar with those names and learn to tune in on the energy of the names. So that's the reason why we only seem to work with a limited number of the Masters.

Also, as well, I have had resistance to working with some Masters. Once in a workshop a woman said to me, "Das, what a fantastic channeler you are. You've inspired so many people in this workshop to channel. Do you ever work with the Master El Morya?" And I said, "El Morya?! Never! I wouldn't work with him if he was the last Master in the whole of creation!" She said, "Why? Das, are you being judgmental?" And I said, "No, just standing in my own power. I won't work with him. He's not my kind of person. He's a disciplinarian. He's serious as hell. I'm not into discipline. I'm into laughter, spontaneity, looning out. Me and him, we just don't hit it off, OK? So, he can get on with his seriousness and I can get on with my fun."

A month or so later there's a letter from Holland, which says, "What a fantastic workshop Das, how much I loved the energy," and everything else. "PS: El Morya told me to tell you that he can be as much of a disciplinarian as you want him to be." When I read that I laughed. So our relationship started to change then. He used the woman to send me the information that he loves me and that I can work with him however I want, a fantastic message of encouragement and empowerment. It kind of loosened me up. I just tell you that to show you that we can also block ourselves in so many other ways. The whole thing is to start making the affirmations, "I am now worthy to start channeling the Lords and Ladies of Shamballa. I am now worthy and willing to channel the Multi-dimensional Masters."

In the early days I was getting everything short of death threats from a Reiki organization and all those kind of people in Europe and Britain, and I was really fed up. I was thinking, "Well I won't bother to do it." As they say in English slang, I was really "on one". One day I'm driving along the freeway in Germany. Since there are no speed limits in Germany, I'm doing about 120, got my stereo banging away, and my phone goes. "Hello Yogi, this is Kuthumi." "What the f— do you want!" was my reply. "My friend, there's certain things that you're not listening to, aren't there?" "Well, what are you doing calling me up on my cell phone!" After a bit of snappy bad-temperedness, I said, "Well, OK, what have you got to tell me?" And Kuthumi said, "You didn't come to earth to be the most popular person, remember that. When you start doing things that people aren't used to, sometimes people get mad with you. There's no problem."

Ann Hughes, who channels Kuthumi, was one of the people who helped to keep everything moving along. One time I was with her, taking a walk, and I asked Kuthumi through her, "What's this system all about?" I was still on about the trouble I was having with the Reiki people, and he said, "You haven't realized, have you, that at this stage, what this is about is connecting people with their I AM Presence, getting people to find out who and what they really are, allowing people to connect with their guidance." And I said, "Yeah, yeah, OK, we'll keep going with that then." Whereas if he'd said, "It's all to do with Reiki, Das," I would have said, "OK, then, that's it! I'm out of here!"

Since the mid-1990's, John has traveled around the world teaching and activating people to the energy of Shamballa. He has been to Iceland, Indonesia, Australia, Mexico, the Congo, Gambia, Cambodia, South Africa, Israel, Egypt, Ireland Tibet, China, Spain, the Netherlands, Bulgaria, Romania, and other places throughout Europe and the USA. Presently he resides in southern France.

I Came to Earth

One day I decided to come to earth,
I thought life would be full of mirth.
Once I arrived I saw a different story:
Illusion had become a form of glory.
My mind said, "Hey boy, what is this?"
My heart said, "I know what it is I miss.
It is the love of the Source for sure,
so how can I become more and more,
OK what to do?" I asked myself,
and the answer was, "Just be yourself.
Don't forget you are an aspect of God Itself.
Be love you are in truth
and then you will be free from the booth
of lies you were told were the truth."
"What are the lies?" I asked myself,
and sometimes they seemed to be so full of wealth.
The thing was though, this was all stealth,
of a plan to get me to deny myself,
Which from now on I will not do,
For Mother-Father God, I am one with you.
Love is, we are, it.
love baba
John Armitage, 2014

CHAPTER 2

MOVING BEYOND REIKI

NEW PARADIGM MDT IS NOT REIKI

Even though it is only a small piece of the original system, Reiki has been a very beautiful way to introduce people to their healing abilities. It is what people were ready for in the early 1900's. In the 1990's, Germain had hoped to make the upward transition (vibrationally speaking) easier by coming in under the Reiki umbrella and then moving on.

John needed a Reiki certificate in order to start teaching what was being called a type of Reiki, so he went to a Reiki master he knew who also was connected with Germain. Germain told her to give John the certificate without the attunements, as the attunements would be restrictive, even debilitating to him. She heard Germain but refused to give John the certification without the attunement. So he agreed to get the attunement, and immediately after he felt his multi-dimensional connections shutting down. He says it took him nine months to find someone to take that attunement off of him, so he could function again as he was used to (now he could easily do it himself).

At that time, there were only a few people in the world who would find the Reiki attunement so restricting, but nowadays that number is growing rapidly. We are ready for more, folks. MUCH more! Germain tells us now that NPMDT is NOT Reiki, and Reiki is NOT NPMDT. Period. Germain says, "I am not 'anti-Reiki'! I founded the original system, after all! It's just that Reiki has moved on, evolved into New Paradigm MDT. This has been the plan all along. The energies that come through NPMDT are *no longer compatible* with the Reiki energy or symbols. These older symbols in your auric field constrict, restrict your frequencies. Nowadays they impede your evolution." This is why, in the NPMDT classes, we do a clearing of all energies we are carrying around in our energy fields that no longer serve us—including activations and initiations from many lifetimes into many systems.

So, clinging to the old symbols is like, as an adult, trying to squeeze yourself into a sweater you wore in first grade. Or like choosing to ride a tricycle up a hill when you have a multi-speed mountain bike available. Why restrict yourself to gears 1-3 when 5th and higher are available to you now?!

A MESSAGE FROM DR. USUI—Channeled through J.A.

It is I, who you know as Usui. It may surprise you that I've been given the honor of speaking with you. To me, it is not really a surprise that I was chosen. For after all, I'm often known as the modern father of this system known as Reiki. Over many years, I've been watching the progress, the re-introduction, the re-integration of the whole energies of Reiki, onto the surface of the planet, amongst the people. It's true that I discovered a small portion of the knowledge that's necessary to successfully utilize this energy known as Reiki. Other parts of what I couldn't find I integrated from my own knowledge, from my own experience. And ultimately it proved to be a system that was working.

Of course, others came later and contorted some of what I said, added to some of what I said, created another restrictive philosophy. I myself did not create a restrictive philosophy. I myself created, or attempted to create, to the best of my ability, a system that would be empowering, freeing! So I always watch closely the progress that the Shamballa [New Paradigm MDT™] family makes, in the re-integration, the re-introduction of these complete energies, of the whole creation. Not only a small aspect of the Universal energy of Reiki, but connections to the whole spectrum of energies available in this moment of Creation.

I admire your bravery, my friends. I admire your fearlessness. For it is the adventurers that always bring new things into the consciousness of others. Understand that you are adventurers of consciousness, explorers of consciousness. Through your adventures, your explorations, the whole of creation will benefit in a most marvelous and wondrous way. So, my friends, may God be with you, each and every one of you. And remember, I am available, any time you may wish to call on me. Bless you.

MOVING BEYOND SYMBOLS

The original healing system brought through by Master Germain in his Atlantean incarnation was represented by 22 symbols. Symbols are two-dimensional representations of multi-dimensional energies. It was a few of these symbols that Dr. Usui discovered and used (along with some Japanese Buddhist symbols) to create the Reiki healing system. Originally Germain's new system was also taught with symbols, Germain having given to Baba a few more of the original ones. Students were taught around 12 or so specific symbols in class, but they were activated to all 352 symbols, one for each of the dimensional levels back to Source. Recently Germain told us to drop the teaching of symbols altogether. He says:

When I asked Baba, or Das as he was known as in those days, to spread the Shamballa energy, I did ask him to use the symbols in the teaching. This was for one reason: to help to focus people's minds and to give the mental something to get hold of. What I did not realize at that time is the way that people would use the symbols to keep themselves in the mental mode, focused on the symbols, and not allow their intuition to work in an allowing way. Of course, this is a broad generalization, as some do this for sure. Some allow the magic to work through them and don't give their power away to the symbols. But keeping the mental mind focused on the symbols, and the mind thinking, " I must use this one and that one," does not allow the energy to flow in an unlimited way. In other words, it limits what can come through you as a channel. Yes, you are a channel if you ground energy.

So this is why I ask now that people give up using and teaching the symbols. As you all know, or should know anyway, that there are 352 symbols in the New Paradigm MDT™ system, and how many were you given? Just a few of them to work with in the mental mode. You were given the rest of the symbols on an energetic level with your activations, and no pictures of them.

The way they work is, you ARE all the symbols, and they work in their own way, because they are God's energy and are therefore intelligent. Easy eh? Just as the energy just is, without using hand positions. On the hand positions: in Usui Reiki I can tell you that Dr Usui did not use them or teach that they should be used. They were invented afterwards, to keep the mental happy as well.

Times were different then, just as they are different now, since the first steps of this system were shared by Baba and me. The energy has moved so fast on the planet that none of us could have imagined. As the energy moves, consciousness moves as well. If we try to stay in the past, we are stuck. The symbols have become a religion to some, and they are used like opium to dull the intuition, thus curtailing freedom, the freedom of the users to allow the magic to flow and work.

So how will we proceed from here? It's easy. From the start, this system has been about connection and freedom: connecting people to their I Am's, and freeing them from the illusion of duality, from being separate, and of course from the illusion of fear. This, of course, allows people to grow and expand. So instead of using symbols in healing, we allow the time that has been spent in trainings, going through the information on symbols and how to use them, to be used instead for people to work with the energy of Shamballa, the energies of the New Paradigm MDT to which they are being activated. Also we can use that time to explain more about the illusion of fear, and so on. The power of self-denial can be explained, as well as the reasons why people get sick and suffer from disease.

How to do the activations without symbols? Again, it's easy. For years now Baba and I have done activations without symbols, both in 13D and the previous levels 1234. The way he does it is, if it's a large group, he just stands up and brings the energy of the activation to everybody. If it's a smaller group, he puts his hands on their heads and just brings it through again the same way. [New Paradigm MDT™ teachers are now taught to create a vortex through which to bring in the activation energies.]

I usually ask him to put his hands on each person for a few seconds, in large groups as well, just to make things more personal. In either case he would just say, "I now bring the energies of [what ever the activation is] and ground it." Some of you have done 13D with us, and you have seen him do it. It's easy, eh? Even in 13D, when I ask him to put his hands on your heads, this is what he says in his mind, " I bless you in the name of the One", three times.

You see, after he has brought the energy of the activation through, it's done. The rest is a bonus. Some say, "Wow that was strong! When you put your hands on me!" Yes of course it is! Blessings in the true sense ARE strong, if you allow them to flow through you.

On the subject of 13D, some think the activations are just connecting people with the 12 dimensions and the energy of the 13th. Yes in some ways it's true, but on a deeper level it is a lot more. Each dimensional level has many different energies in it, so the activation tunes your energy system to allow these energies to flow through you. These activations are personal for each individual; each one gets what they are ready for, under the guidance of their own I Am Presence.

So that's it, really. No doubt Baba will have some emails about all this, and that's fine. Some will stick to the old way, and that's fine as well. All is perfect in the eyes of God. Myself, I am looking to bringing a new level of empowerment and freedom into things, hence my request not to make New Paradigm MDT™ teaching a focus on the external representation of energy in the form of symbols. I AM Germain. Namaste.

CHAPTER 3

WHAT IS *MULTI-DIMENSIONAL TRANSFORMATION?*

YOUR MULTI-DIMENSIONAL SELF

What exactly do we mean by "multi-dimensional"? We in the Western world are used to thinking in only 3 dimensions. When we talk about our "bodies" we are usually referring to the three-dimensional, seemingly solid body that we walk around in, that bumps into tables occasionally, and that sometimes "gets sick" and doesn't function so well. Western medicine doctors and researchers, for the most part, deal only with this physical vehicle of five recognized senses: sight, smell, taste, touch, and hearing. The very term "scientific method" requires that something be measurable within the third dimension and these recognized senses, in order to be acknowledged as legitimate. Of course, physicists have discovered fairly recently that the results of all experiments are affected by the observer, and that there are at least 11 dimensions "out there" [actually 12 available to humans at this time], but this knowledge has yet to convince the majority of people in today's science fields to reconsider their current conception of "the scientific method" and its possible inadequacies and limitations.

The spirit, or soul, is mysterious, and not everyone even believes that they have one. Something seems to "leave" at death, and then the body no longer functions and begins to decay, or break back down to the earth elements of which it is composed. Western doctors have become very adept at dealing with chemical abnormalities and other symptoms of disease, and at cutting out diseased and malfunctioning parts. Anything else has been relegated to the status of religion and myth. Only recently are Western medical people starting to understand how the mind is intimately connected to the physical body and its health; a few are beginning to find out that, to a great extent, what we think is who we are and how we function, how we get sick and how we heal.

The mind is more than the brain. The physical brain is a computer through which the mind can manifest. To restrict all knowledge to that which one can fully understand through the five senses that we recognize is very limiting, indeed. Master Germain has told us that, even while living in these bodies, we have access to 12 senses; the other seven are shut down, or dormant, in most people. Some are starting to awaken to their multi-dimensional senses, such as clairvoyance, clairsentience, clairaudience. It is useful to know that you have them, and that they are a normal part of your being, when this begins to happen!

Eastern science has been aware of the multi-dimensionality of our beings for a long time. Many of the terms they use come from Sanskrit, a very ancient language. For example, *chakras* ("spinning wheels") are the energy centers of the body, through which life force flows into the physical body. This is how we can be a spiritual being having a 3D physical experience on earth.

Chakras also serve as transformers, toning down the vibrations of the life force from Creator/Source, so that is usable by our lower-vibrational 3D body. The *antahkarana* is a tube of light that runs through the center of the body, connecting the major chakras and grounding the body into the earth. As we open to our multi-dimensional senses, we also expand our consciousness to flow up from our crown chakra, through this antahkarana, through the many higher dimensions of our Self, all the way to Creator.

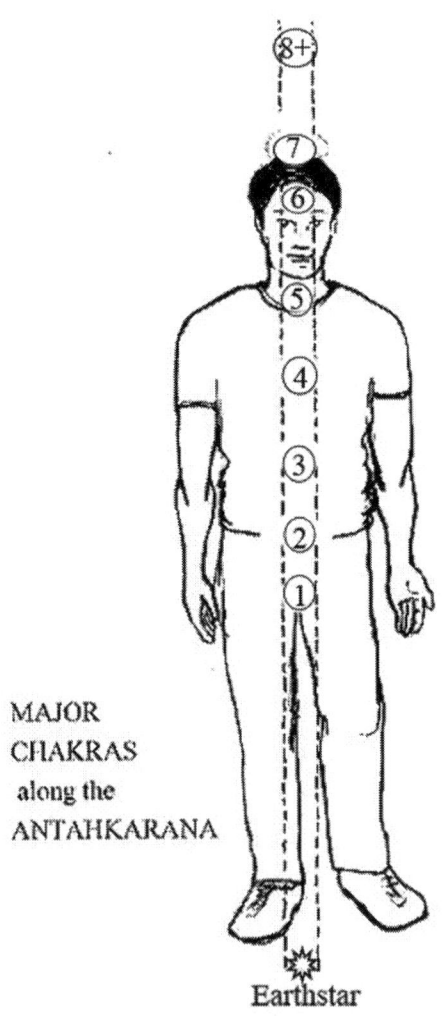

MAJOR
CHAKRAS
along the
ANTAHKARANA

Earthstar

Major Chakras along the Antahkarana

We open to the higher aspects of our own Self and are able to hear their advice. We don't have to follow this guidance. We still have free will, to take as long as we wish on the path back to consciousness of our own God/Goddess nature, and to have adventures and all kinds of experiences along the way. Sometimes as well, being in a physical body, we may have a different perspective on something than our multi-dimensional helpers, who may not have been in body for a very long time. We need to treat them as part of a team, of which we ourselves are also an integral part. Indeed, in terms of our own process here on earth, each of us is the chairperson of his or her own team. Still, I know from experience that it is usually best to listen to your own I Am Presence, and to consider very carefully if you decide on a different path than that it is suggesting. All is experience.

We are electro-magnetic beings. Shakespeare got it when he said, "We are such stuff as dreams are made on" (*The Tempest*). In a very real sense, this personality walking around on earth in a physical body, that I usually think of as "me," is really a holographic projection from my I Am Presence, experiencing life on earth in order to expand Creator's knowledge of Itself. "What a piece of work is a man! How noble in reason! How infinite in faculties! In form and moving how express and admirable! In action how like an angel! In apprehension how like a god! The beauty of the world, the paragon of animals!" Shakespeare again, *Hamlet*. It's no accident that I quote Shakespeare, for Master Germain was author of these plays, in his life as Francis Bacon. We are amazing beings, and our physical bodies no less so than the rest.

These physical bodies are only made possible by a series of higher dimensional bodies. Electricity leaves the power station through large cables, moving through transformer boxes in order to be able to travel through smaller wires, and again another transformer to smaller wires, until finally it reaches your house. If this did not happen, the high voltage of the original electricity would burn out the wiring in your home, rather than power your lights and machines. So do these etheric bodies around your physical body gradually transform the energies of creation down to a vibrational level compatible with 3D manifestation.

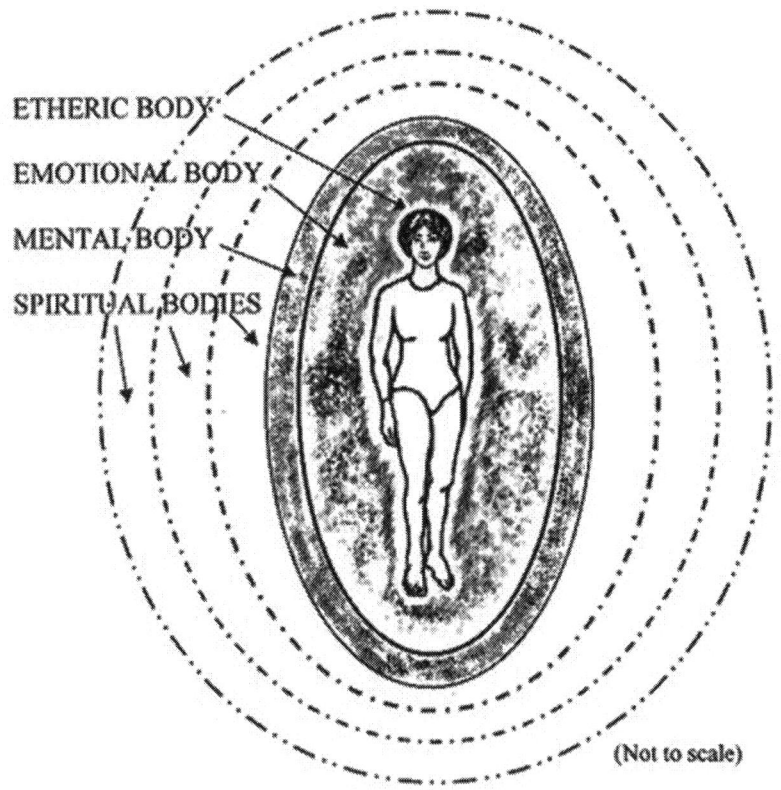

ETHERIC BODY

EMOTIONAL BODY

MENTAL BODY

SPIRITUAL BODIES

(Not to scale)

Our Multi-Dimensional Bodies

Surrounding the physical body is what psychic seers see as a network of blue lines of energy. This serves as the pattern or blueprint for the physical body. We call these lines of energy *meridians*. This *etheric body* is the reason that amputees can sometimes still feel their lost limb; the pattern for that limb is still there. Meridians are well known to practitioners of acupuncture and acupressure, as well as practitioners of all vibrational forms of healing. This includes homeopathic remedies, flower essences and gem elixirs, sounding and chanting, and remote or hands-on "energy work."

Next are the *emotional body* (extending around 8" out when at rest), and the *mental body* (extending around 24" out from the physical body), followed by a series of *spiritual bodies*. Each body is of a higher vibration than the one before it, moving up from 3D, the physical, to Source. The bodies interpenetrate each other, but are separated by dimension and membrane. They are connected through the major chakras, which are located in the central axis of the body. Different cultures have had different names and concepts of the configuration of these etheric bodies, but essentially all agree that they are there, whatever they are called by our 3D minds.

Most disease originates as thought (electro-magnetic in origin), which, if not brought back into balance, moves down vibrationally into emotion. Then, if this energy is not released, it continues to move down in frequency until it affects the functioning of the physical body. Our thoughts and emotions, to a very great extent, determine the state of our health. Treating physical symptoms with chemical substances can only affect such problems in the physical. Drugs leave the original cause untreated. We can achieve some physical comfort from pharmaceuticals, but only we, ourselves, can initiate true healing, by changing our attitudes. In this effort, the vibrational or energetic methods and remedies can prove very useful.

When we release fear and all of it's manifestations—such as anger, despair, anxiety, hatred—we start on the road to wellness, to balance and mastery. The universe is created of Love without conditions; anything else is illusion. Humans are very good at creating and believing in illusion. Fortunately, Love and fear cannot exist in the same place at the same time, so filling oneself with Love without conditions can help us to release our debilitating fears. Love without conditions is not an emotion; it is a state of being. It is our *true* state of being.

I know from experience that this is so. I was raised as a fundamentalist Christian. My father was a fundamentalist minister. Fundamentalist means simply following a strict set of beliefs. Anyone living outside of the box of beliefs of that particular persuasion is considered wrong, misguided, or in extreme cases, infidel and non-human. These are, of course, man-made beliefs created from fear and a deep sense of inadequacy. There are fundamentalists in all the religions. There are even New Age fundamentalists (adhering to strict rules, perhaps about not eating certain things like meat, smoking, etc.). Fundamentalism is exclusionary. Mother-Father God/Creator/All-That-Is is inclusive, all loving, without judgment.

My father was a very loving man with very violent beliefs. He would give his last cent to someone who seemed to need it (no matter their belief system), but he believed fervently that non-believers (those who did not believe according to what he was taught and held as the "Truth") were going to a fiery hell. Towards the end of his life, as he got sicker and sicker, he was terrified of dying. He did not know for certain that he was "saved". I was with him during the last few hours of his life, sitting by his bed in the hospital, surrounding him with the energy of Love. He was not conscious, but I felt his presence.

The next morning, around 3 AM, I received a call that he had died. Immediately we felt him in the room with us. He was very happy. He told us, "It's so different from what I expected! All Creation is made up of LOVE, Love without conditions!" He had expected judgment, the illusion that humans in fear and guilt had created about how the universe functions. He had found the real thing, Love. He was ecstatic. He told us he was now off to "make amends" to some people he felt he had harmed by his restrictive belief system.

My father is a wonderful example of how we create our illnesses through fear, and how these thoughts and emotions, which are originally held in our other-dimensional bodies, are the true cause of most dis-ease in our 3D bodies. He also shows us that we can break through the illusion and heal ourselves. He was able on his death to accept the Love he was offered, probably because of the loving heart he had held in life. We can also break through this illusion of fear and heal ourselves during our lifetime, before we leave 3D, by releasing the fear and accepting Love without conditions, without judgment, into our entire being. This is healing on a multi-dimensional level. This is what New Paradigm Multi-Dimensional Transformation™ is about. Shamballa energies help us to release the old, low vibrational energies that we have been holding on to for lifetimes, energies that have been holding us back from knowing who we truly are.

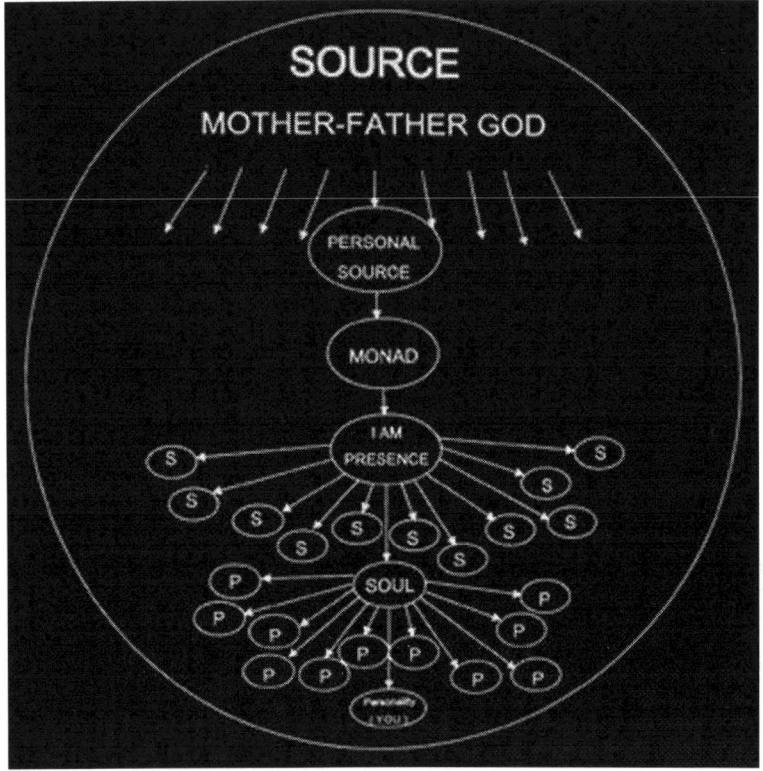

Where you are in the scheme of things.

Who are we? We are Love. We are created of the very substance of Creator/Mother-Father God/All-That-Is, and this is Divine Love. This is Divine Light. It cannot be anything else! As we release the old, false belief systems and energies, we learn to love ourselves, to love ourselves as Mother/Father, God/Goddess-All-That-Is loves us, without judgment, without conditions. We learn to love others without judgment, to see and allow others their own path. We open to Love, we open to Joy. We begin to live in a higher vibrational state of being. Eventually this leads us to merge our personality self with our higher Self, or I Am Presence. This is called *ascension*. Nowadays this does not mean floating off into the sky; it means walking a new path on *the earth*, a path of Love without judgment.

The earth is rising dimensionally, going through her own ascension process. The earth is a great being, a sentient being. Our physical bodies are made up of her substance, so she is truly our Mother. As she goes through this ascension process, through 4th dimension and eventually into 5th and higher, we can go along with her, but only if we let go of all of the lower vibrational energies that we have held on to for so long. As we raise our vibrational rate, these lower energies start to kick up a fuss. If we allow ourselves to fall back into these old memories, feelings, and habits, we may become anxious, have strange dreams, become fearful. Knowing is half the battle. Doing is the rest. Let it go, breathe, allow yourself to shift into Love.

In New Paradigm MDT classes, everyone is led through clearing meditations, before being infused with the higher energies that have been made available to us for our spiritual growth. Each person gets what he or she is ready and willing to receive, under the guidance, always, of their own I Am Presence, and according to what they are willing to release. They are also taught how to take responsibility for their own lives, which is what is meant by "walking the path of mastery". A *master* is simply one who is Master of his/her own Self.

FACILITATING HEALING FOR OTHERS—J.A.

As the founder of New Paradigm MDT, I have always asked that people send healing on request only, or first to ask the I Am Presence, or higher Self of the person concerned for permission. I also say though, that if you decide to send any healing whatsoever, it should be in accordance with Divine Will and the will of each person's I Am.

I learned many years ago that including my will into the equation is not the way to go. I used to do healing sessions and always had a desire of the outcome. My ego told me I was good. My ego was happy with itself, because it thought I was good. But at one period in my life, I was into willing people, willing their bodies into changes. I was generating karma with the people, interfering with their life streams. It seemed like I was working miracles. People would come knocking on the door looking for healing. I was famous, working miracles. But some people would come back in a few months. People with seriously bad backs would come, and 45 minutes later they would walk away. I would actually will them to come into alignment. They would say, "It's a miracle!"

Not everybody came back, but enough to get me to question. They'd say, "You know, you fixed me a few months ago. It was a miracle! Can you do it again, please?" There's a cause for every effect in this. In general, unless it's manifested by our I Am Presence to give us a lesson in what we have to learn, we've actually created our illnesses ourselves. People don't realize we've actually created our own disease, by the way that we think, our emotions, the way we relate to life and so on. This is how we manifest our own disease. It's not sensible to will people's bodies to do something. This is why I've been saying for years that there is no such thing as healers, only facilitators. People heal themselves. We just facilitate the situation so as to allow them to heal themselves. It was a big lesson for me.

Then a lady helped me learn the lesson, along with [multi-dimensional master] Kuthumi. I got a call one day to go see this lady. She was dying in the chair. The doctor had said she was dying. People are selfish, they don't want people to die. I said, "I don't allow them to die! Get back in there!" She woke up, all perky. I felt very happy and proud of myself. A couple days later I went back to give her another dose. Everybody's sad. "Where is she?" "She's dead." "What! She was perky as anything two days ago, when we finished with her!" My ego was angry.

It was this incident that triggered Kuthumi to talk with me. He'd been watching me, thinking, "When will he learn?" Because sometimes the Upstairs Department and our Helpers just observe us, wondering how long it will take for us to realize. He told me, "You are interfering with the person's free will here. You should allow them to heal themselves, if they want to. You provide the energy, and they heal or not; you are not the healer, just the medium for the energy."

Even now, sometimes I have these "bang" realizations in other areas of my life; I call them "baseball bat realizations"—because it hits you straight in the head. "That's so obvious! Why didn't I think of that in the last 60 years!" But often our Helpers, our I Am Presences, just let us carry on, have the adventure, go through the process. This is the way you're going to learn. There wouldn't be any point in reincarnating if our I Am Presences, the angels and archangels, the multidimensional Masters and so on were going to keep saying to us, "Do this. Do that. Do the other thing. Turn right, turn left, eat that piece of bread." I mean, there wouldn't be any point, would there? There'd be no adventure in life. It would be dead boring. No challenges. "Go away, let me make some mistakes, have an adventure!"

Don't interfere with free will. We don't have the permission to do that. Just allow the energy to flow through you. If you send to the I Am Presence of the person without permission, it is wise to put in the command, "If you don't want it, send it on to somebody who does." Who needs karma with people? Nobody. Of course there are ways of avoiding karma, but that's another tale.

Remember, doing good works for so called good karma is as undesirable as so-called bad karma. We are working on being free now, not stacking up more things to sort out.

ON MULTI-DIMENSIONAL DISEASE—J.A.

Disease is a multi-dimensional manifestation of something. Where disease is concerned, there's no hard and fast rule about how the disease manifests into the physical, or into the mental faculties attached to the physical. Disease has many trigger points, many different types of triggers. On the third dimensional level, it could have to be with defective nutrition, with total denial of who you are, etc., and you actually want to get out of it. Parkinson's is a bit like that. Usually there you find people who don't want to be here; they're not totally present, they've never enjoyed themselves here. They may be arch controllers, but in the end they discover that none of this works, and they're afraid to kill themselves, so they manifest "I'm not here." The lights are on, but nobody's home. But a lot of abnormal behavior is caused by multiple occupancy of the body. Once you learn to communicate on an I Am Presence level, it becomes simple. You just ask the I Am Presence of the person what's going on, and listen to the answer.

There are so many different things happening in our world, and in other dimensional realities. I've been facilitating healing since I was a small boy, and I'd always known that disease manifests first in the emotional, in the astral bodies, and then works its way down to the physical. That's where the doctors fall short in their treatments; they don't treat the cause, only the symptoms. But I never realized, as well, that there's multi-dimensional disease, that disease can be manifest in many dimensional realities. It could be manifest in the eighth dimension, or the seventh, and then it falls down eventually into the third/fourth. We have a body that equates to each dimension. We are actually experiencing in a body in every dimensional reality, up to twelve—some even higher now. So you can have disease in other dimensional realities that actually also starts to manifest here, in the physical. So it's not quite as simple to explain as our human conscious minds would like it to be. But when you work with guidance, it becomes dead simple. There's nothing too much to work out.

One of the problems we have with our ego-driven conscious mind is that it wants to know the ins and outs of everything, to put everything into a box or pigeonhole. That's impossible. Creation is complex. It's not that it's incomprehensible, it's that everything affects everything in creation. The only way we can get to the bottom of it all is to work with our guidance. Your 3D ego mind can't comprehend, in many ways, or easily, how you even work with your guidance. The information often that you're given in guidance, your conscious mind says, "What?!" Just get out of the way, so we can do the job. Just allow rather than control. Humans think they have to control everything. No, you have to *allow* everything, not control.

Here is my piece on the whole thing. Those who have workshopped with me over the years have heard me rave about this, over and over again. The bottom line of my thoughts and guidance on this is as follows. First, remember the W.H.O. of the U.N., the F.D.A., and in England, the Department of Health and Social Security, from now on known as the Department of Stealth and Total Obscurity, and the drug companies are all hand in hand of this one. Money and control is the game here. How? Well it's easy to understand, and the world management team is hand in hand with all this as well.

"OH yeah!!" I hear you say, "not another conspiracy." No, not another one, but fact. What fact? Easy really. First, if you are sick, you are not whole. We could go on for hours about not being whole, but let's keep it short. If your immune system is not in good order, you get sick, viruses and so on invade, and your system has all kinds of effects. If you don't know about natural health and healing and so on, what do you do? Go off to the doctor.

"Well doc, I am sick." "OK, never mind, take these pills, you will be OK." Pills cost money, and the doc as well. It's easy to understand, the kind of money they make, if amazing. The costs of the drugs are mostly less than pennies but sell for many dollars each, and they dish out billions of 'em, big bucks.

Add to it the antibiotics, well its gets better if you are a drug company. Give the people lots of 'em, nuke their bodies, and kill everything in their guts and bowel. Ah, now they can't produce the things they need to survive, can't absorb minerals and so on, so they get sicker and are always being invaded by more bugs. More doctors visits and pills and maybe even hospital, more money. In the UK over 50% of people in hospital are in there because of taking pills from the doc; go to hospital in the UK and be invaded by some super bug! Happens all the time; 5000 people or more die from it here every year as well; good for the pocket.

OK, I agree it's all choice, but for many, they don't know, so they can't choose. They just go with the "gods", the doctors. For sure, it is the new religion, going to the doctors and being processed. Me, I was worried the new religion was NPMDT! LOL

It is said that vaccination has killed off some viruses or whatever that make us sick. Yes, we don't have cholera in the UK and mainland Europe and America and places, and TB the same. Why? We have clean water and mainly dry housing, with heating and fridges to keep our food in. So why is TB on the increase in Europe? We are supposed to be safe from it with jabs. Why do loads of kids get measles, if they are jabbed against it?

Evolution is the key here, and the activation times we have when we go through childhood disease process. Nowadays, people never have the fevers and the other things that go with these invasions, and the boost our immune system gets from these times. The fevers connect us with our I Am and Source and activate our light bodies. What happens through that? It makes us aware of the choices we have in front of us in our lives, and it helps us to follow our guidance. So, another reason why the controllers don't want us to have these childhood things.

We are told our kids will die if they don't have the vaccinations, and rubbish like that. I can tell you, my kids have all had measles, and they are alive and strong; they have had other childhood things as well. I just sat with them and gave them healing and [homeopathic] remedies as they needed them, no doctor or drugs. Of course, it's scary if you don't know what to do, I agree. For me though, I like to keep out of the clutches of doctors, if possible.

I remember when I had cancer a few years back, a few very funny things happened. When I announced to our e-list that I had cancer, people wrote all kinds of things to me. The sensible ones asked if I could have the time to do one last workshop with them before I left. Some said, "Good luck Baba, I hope you make it, and I am sending you healing energy." But some said, "You need to see a doctor!!!!" Well, that was a few years ago. I had been given nine months to live by the Upstairs Department, unless I decided to heal myself! Still here, though, and did not see a doctor. To me, doing that would have been denying all I live for, freedom and choice.

So what is the upshot of all this stuff? Of course, all I have written above, but there is more to it. The main reason people seem to shout about jabs is because of the mercury and what it does to the body. They seem to forget about the rest of the health stuff, like asthma, and skin disorders, and stomach and bowel problems caused by the jabs. And of course, people focus on the problems, or so-called problems with the mind, AHD and ADHD, dyslexia and so on. For me, I wonder if it's a bad thing having those things. Yes, it makes life hard at school, for sure. I know it, because I have so-called AHD and dyslexia myself, even today. When I left school I could not read and write and so on.

But is that bad, I ask myself? At least I have been able to connect with the angels and helpers all my life and not been conditioned into the social norm. Yes, more trouble I guess, having suffered, or should I say experienced, addictions and such, and even jail for not being "normal", as well as a spell in the madhouse because I told doctors I could heal my wife if they stopped drugging her, back in the 70's. But still, I am glad I am like this.

I see, in many ways, that the plan is starting to backfire on the controllers here, just like the radiation plan did. People are becoming more aware through so called dyslexia and AHD. These kids cause problems at school, of course, because they see through the plans to brainwash them into obedient clones, and rebel against it. What is needed is special education for these people, into the true nature of life in this universe. Of course, this will take time, but believe me, it will happen for sure. Meanwhile, the drug companies will work at getting the governments to make laws against energy healing and natural remedies, because they are losing out on mega bucks when people are healing themselves. In places like Africa, where I work, the first thing we do is give everybody homeopathic remedies to reverse the vaccinations they have had, and then afterwards get on with the health problems they have.

I do believe that we all come to earth to make some kind of difference here. Some come to be the mapmakers. Often the mapmakers have a hard time. No need really to go into that, just look into history. So what is the bottom line in all of this? Follow your heart and be free, that's all. Make your own choices and follow them. Life is an adventure; treat it as such. And be aware that your choices are being taken from you under your very nose.

CHAPTER 4

BECOMING MASTER OF YOUR SELF

Stepping into your Mastery is an opportunity to step out of the childhood state (feeling powerless, a potential victim needing outside protection by some all-powerful Deity against some evil energy "out there") to become fully adult, in the spiritual sense: heart fully open in Love without conditions, listening to and being guided by the Divine Presence within, the I Am Presence. Mastery means simply being a master of one's Self. We will keep repeating that. It means taking full responsibility for oneself and one's life. It means dropping the blinders and blindfolds with which humanity has limited and constricted itself for so long, to step into limitless freedom and joy. It means consciously walking the path of limitless Being, knowing that this is the birthright of all humans, if they but open to it. It means the buck stops here.

MASTERY—Master Germain, channeled by J.A.

Many of you know, and the rest are starting to realize, that mastery is not having a bit of paper [certificate] that says you're a master. All a piece of paper does, that says you're a master, is to remind you to work on your mastery. Another thing it does is to make other people, that maybe come to you for teaching, advice, or healing feel that this person knows what they're doing, because they have a piece of paper here that says they're a master.

Mastery has nothing to do with a piece of paper. Mastery has to do with life. Mastery is to do with sovereignty: sovereignty over your life, sovereignty over your energy, sovereignty over your creations. For by now, you should all know that you are, each and every one of you, creators and co-creators. Let's look at creatorship. Now, each and every one of you has the potential to create worlds, create universes, create ecosystems. Think about that. Let that information pass through your conscious mind. Let that information start to sit, as a memory, in your cellular structure.

By now you could be thinking, "How could I do this?" For many, at this moment, it is not a viable project or proposition. That isn't a judgment, it's a reminder that you're not accepting who and what you are, each and every one of you in this moment. Each and every one of you is god and goddess NOW. Every one of you, every sub-atomic particle, every microtron and super electron, is a carbon copy of the whole of creation. As above, so below, Sananda [Jesus] said in his Palestinian ministry. He was trying to remind you of who and what you are.

So as of this moment, if you haven't integrated your god- and goddess-ness, how can we help you to do that? Well, we can push you, pull you, cajole you into stepping out of the constraints of your present consciousness, out of the self-imposed constraints of doubt and fear, into a place of mastership, beauty, harmony, and abundance. For as I said, mastership is not about a piece of paper, it is about life, about love, about understanding that you are the creator of your life in this moment, and the co-creator of what is happening in all of creation at this moment. When you look outside yourselves, and you see something that sparks your inner fire, which sparks this thing that many would know as temper, anger, those kinds of reactions, understand that that thing which you say that you don't like, and you judge, on one level you helped to create it.

How so? If you believe that there is one Source of all life, one Creator, then everything in life, everything that happens, must be part of that Life, that One. If you trust in the process of life, in divine timing with no accidents; if you believe that every experience you have is your opportunity to demonstrate your mastery; and if you believe that your life essence is eternal, how can you judge yourself, an event, the choice or action of another person, as right, wrong, good, bad, or as anything other than an expression of the One?

So then you allow every experience to unfold magically in front of you. And as it unfolds magically in front of you, to accept the magic, allowing the magic to be in your life, to be in your hearts, to be in your minds. Take a few moments to think upon my words. Some of you have pieces of paper to say that you are masters. I would like each and every one of you to think now how you are using your mastery in your lives.

STANDING IN YOUR POWER—J.A.

I say, if it's happening to me, it's happening to me. I don't ask, "Is this all right?" That's disempowering myself. I don't ask anything outside of myself if something is all right. Because that actually means that I consider somewhere in my consciousness, no matter how deep down it's hidden in my cellular structure, that I'm a victim of something, and that I am not actually in control of my reality. So people ask, "How do you protect yourself?" Well, I never protect myself, because I AM divine protection. Because I'm not a victim. It's all about changing the way that we think, and standing in our own power. Although the others, the Elohim and the masters and the other billions of them hanging out in multi-dimensional reality can aid us, we should never give our power away to them. So I never say, "Is this all right?" I make up my mind. Is this in accord with the will of my I Am Presence? "Hey, I Am Presence, is this cool?" "Sure, Baba, it's cool." I never ask the Elohim, "Is this cool?"—because then I'm giving my power away to them.

Again, people ask, "How do you protect yourself?" Well, I never protect myself, because I AM divine protection. Not "I NEED divine, protection" but "I AM divine protection". By saying "I AM divine protection", I say that I understand that I am in charge of my own reality. I'm not a victim of anything. It's only my ego that might try to convince me that I need protection or that I'm a victim. As soon as you say, "I need protection," it means that you're not standing in your power. It's an affirmation of standing out of your power. It's an affirmation of, "I'm a victim. Come and get me! Whatever's looking for mischief, come and play mischief with me!" Notice that I didn't say "do something bad" or anything like that, because that's judgment too. If you're out for mischief, and someone here says, "I'm a victim and I need protection,"—"Ha-ha! Well we can play mischief here, because this person's not in their power!"

The last time that some of our star brothers said, "We're going to take you away and finish you off!" I just rolled a cigarette and said, "Well, why do you think you can do that? Why do you think that I'm going to allow it?!" I didn't say, "My God, I need divine protection!" I said, "I AM divine protection. Why are you messing with me? You should know this." It's a whole different way of looking at things. It's understanding that, when you stand in your own power, you ARE all that there is. We are all that there is. Our conditioning as human beings is *so strong*, that people find it very, very hard sometimes to stop giving their power away to things outside of themselves. So stop giving your power away to anything but your own I Am Presence.

I remember years ago, I was driving along a road in the country in southwest England, down a narrow little valley with a river running through, and I see this UFO coming down the valley. I start communicating with them, "Hey, who are you folk?" "Hey, we're coming to take you away, ha-ha!" So they land in the field, my car stops, the lights go out. You know, typical close encounter of the third kind business.

I get out of my car, thinking, "Bloody hell. I'm going to need a bit of help here." They're saying to me, "We're going to take you!" Somewhere in the back of my mind it's saying, "I wonder if they can?" I wasn't standing in my own power. So I say, "Kali come and help me!" So the goddess Kali appears. They say, "What do you want?!" She says, "I'm looking after him." They say, "Well, we want him!" She says, "You can't have him!" They say, "Why not?" She says, "Because I love him." So they left.

In those days I wasn't completely standing in my own power. I'd call on [Archangel] Michael, or Kali, or the others I was used to giving away my power away to. Now I'd maybe say, if I really felt I could use a bit of help, "Hey Kali, fancy giving me a hand here?" instead of "Hey Kali, I need you!" Just "fancy giving me a little backup?" It's all a question of understanding that, when you're in your mastery, nothing can happen to you in this way. That's why you don't need protection. It's all designed to keep reinforcing the disempowerment in your own mind, to stop you from standing in your own power. "I need protection!" You're actually saying, "I consider I'm a piece of shit. I'm nothing!" It's like the old thing, "Oh, God help me!" God says, "Why, do you want to give your power away?" But if you say, "I'm doing, and maybe you can give me a hand?" God says, "Well great! This person's doing, and I will give them a hand."

It's so deep in the consciousness, so deep in the cellular structure, the programming in the DNA, "Give your power away, give your power away. You're a victim, you're a victim, you're a victim. You can't stand in your own power." This is what we're working on getting over. That's another part of the workshops that we do, getting over this programming that there's nothing you can do. Because you can actually do everything! Everything, in a second! Everything in a second, if you integrate the fact that you can.

God helps them that help themselves, it is true. But if you don't help yourself, you don't get anything. God isn't going to come along and say, "You know, you're a miserable piece of dirt, and I'm going to pull you out into your own power." What God, or what Yahweh says to you as a human being (most people think Yahweh's God anyway), what Yahweh says to you is, "I created you in my own image. You have the *adam cadmon* light body of perfection, you have a copy of my light body, which is capable of linking with All-That-Is, and capable of understanding that there's no separation in duality. If you want to keep on interacting with the illusion of separation in duality, in third dimensional reality, you're free to do it as long as you want." It's only through this illusion of separation in duality do we as human beings go into these feelings of disempowerment and separation and thinking that you are not Mother/Father God, because you ARE.

So part of what this work is about in these workshops is getting you to this frame of mind, "Yes, I am all powerful! When I say energy moves, it does!" That's how I bring the energies down. That's how I work with the Teams clearing out your implants, because I say so. No special skills. I never went to a school for a hundred years to learn this, and got a certificate. The stuff I'm working with now isn't even in books, so I didn't read it in a book. I've been doing my work over my lifetime by integrating different aspects of standing in my own power, and understanding that when I say energy moves, it does. And more and more I understand that. I didn't integrate it all in one go, and I still don't claim in this moment to have completely integrated it into my conscious mind now. I'm also taking steps, like you are, in integration.

I Am on Earth

One day I realized as I looked around,
my feet were firmly on the ground.
I looked some more, round and round,
and saw the beauty all around.
Don't follow the illusion of mind,
take yourself away from the daily grind.
Look inside and there you will find
a true you beyond what you think you are,
shining like a really bright star,
lighting the universe with you are that you are,
just Love Divine no more no less.
Life is not a real mess,
don't let yourself go down under stress.
It is about love and being, no more or less.
The rest is an adventure,
so don't be afraid to venture
outside the box, for life really rocks
if you just let go of the blocks,
not blocks for buildings but the ones we build.
If we just let life rock,
our hearts say yes,
we are out of this mess,
into the memory of we are all one,
love flows and the Divine plan lives,
in all our hearts.
Our illusion never outsmarts
the seed of love that creates all things,
the love of Source is the Source of Love,
so now let's link below with above,
connect with our true selves,
bring it to our world,
and just be.
love all serve all baba
John Armitage, 2014

WHAT IS THE EGO?

A master is one who awakens and listens to the internal voice of Truth, of the I Am Presence, and orders his or her life accordingly. But how do we distinguish the voice of Truth from the voice of illusion? The voice of illusion, of the personality, or ego self, is very loud and often drowns out the I Am Presence, which speaks from the silence within. Unless you can learn to recognize this strident voice of falsity of the ego, it takes over your life. Your sense of Self gets mixed up with the form that you are temporarily inhabiting.

What is the ego? When souls began inhabiting physical bodies, originally the ego served a specific small function: that of survival of the physical body. The ego functions out of FEAR, fear that originally got you to run away from a saber tooth tiger, perhaps. But as we became entranced by the physical senses and lost connection with our greater Self, through the density of form, the ego began to take on a role for which it was not suited. It began to run the whole show. As it was not capable to do this, it rapidly became insane.

The ego lives and feeds on anxiety, fear, anger, resentment, all the emotions and thoughts of separation. It is constantly putting itself forward and trying to make others seem less, through defining that separation as much as it can. It needs to feel "special" and better than others (or if not that, then worse than others—you know, "I'm BAAD!"), to reinforce its difference. It is very serious about itself. Even attachment to "spirituality", in the sense that one feels "above all that" or better than others, is a sign of the ego.

One of the greatest weapons against the ego is humor: become aware of yourself being lost in the illusions of the ego, and laugh at yourself. Awareness is the first step. Baba once gave us the image of the masters in the Upstairs Department, as he calls it, rolling on the floor with laughter at the strange actions and reactions of humans. This image often helps me to see and be able to laugh at my own foibles, as well as those of the society I live in. NOT REACTING to the ego in others, not getting caught up in their dramas, is often the best way to help them move beyond this insanity.

The ego can interfere with what you are doing in the present moment. It only exists in the past (and anxieties about the future, based on past experiences), so the present makes it nervous. It tries to switch you into *looking at* yourself instead of *being in* yourself. For instance, sometimes when I am channeling, the ego voice of "you can't do this" or "what makes you think this is real?" comes into my consciousness and begins to interfere with my multi-dimensional connection. When I feel my ego trying to knock me out of the moment, I create in my thoughts a box filled with pink light, Love without conditions. I put an image of the ego-self into this box, or cell, and let it bliss out, while I continue on with what I was doing. This can work quite well.

The aim of New Paradigm MDT™ is to help people to stand in their own power, firmly connected to their own I Am Presence (and keeping their ego in check). Discerning the difference between the advice of the I Am Presence and that of your ego is a part of mastery. It really isn't difficult. Your ego wants you to be (or appear) "special" and better than others (or sometimes worse than others); your I Am isn't interested in this, only with getting the job done. The job is helping people connect to their own I Am Presence and stand in their own power. (The best manual on ego-management I have found is Eckhart Tolle's book, *A New Earth*, Namaste Publishing, Plume, Penguin Group, 2006. NY-USA, London-England, Toronto-Canada, Victoria-Australia, New Delhi-India, Auckland-New Zealand, Johannesburg-S. Africa.)

THE INSANE EGO—J.A. & Germain channeled by J.A.

Before you read this, I would ask you to get your ego in a straight line, a straight line behind you (smile). Germain and I are going to tell you a bit about ego. The first thing we need to understand is that our true self is not the ego. The ego is an insane being who may have convinced us that we, our true selves, are it. It is not true.

The thing is, the insane ego is a being or entity who tells us that it is the true us. This being tells us we are victims and are at the mercy of all things. It tells us "think through the left brain, this is the place that shows us the truth." I can tell you, this is not true, although you may be convinced by this entity that it is true.

The only way we can see truth is through our hearts, in love. This means we don't judge, we don't process about the perceived threats to our being. The real truth is that there are no threats except the ones perceived by this insane entity the ego. For all is love. Live through the heart, and you will see this in action. Who needs to judge? Nobody but the insane ego.

Let me tell you a bit more. This being who has convinced you that you *are* it lives in total fear. WHY? Easy one this, because it is in fear of being found out. It will keep you running around in circles, "I need to be right, I need to control all aspects of life, I need to be me, the presence in 3D, me, the one who has needs."

Believe us in truth, no one has needs beyond Divine love. This is all we need. Remember the Biblical saying, "an eye for an eye"? If we go on like this, it means the whole world becomes blind. Let's give the world our love, just that, seeing the perfection of the Divine in all. Please let God hug you, feel the Source through your heart, and LIVE in this Divine love and allowance.

If you are not happy with anything, just change it in this love. What else to do, fight? Well, the insane ego may try to convince you this is the way, but the only worthwhile fight is the fight with the destructive self. Even then, LOVE will save you lifetimes in this process, for fight and struggle are also an illusion. Remember who you are, and be that.

GIVING AWAY YOUR POWER—J.A. and a spokesperson of the Confederation of Free Worlds (channeling is in italics)

There is one thing that I feel the need to be said here. It is a very important message, not only for the people in this room but also for everybody on planet Earth. The basis of this message is: Never, never, ever try to give your power away to something outside of yourself.

There seems to be an idea in the collective consciousness on planet Earth, through conditioning, that there is always something or somebody outside of yourself that knows everything. It is not true. It is another thing happening upon the planet in order to keep the energy of disempowerment in the consciousness of the people. There is this huge movement that seems to be building again on the planet. This movement, we should call it a modern form of disempowerment. I would call it the cult of the Ascended Masters. People have a tendency to believe that the Ascended Masters know everything, that they are perfect in every way, that they have access to all the knowledge and energy in the whole of creation. It is not true. The Ascended Masters will be the first people to tell you it is not true. Where organized religion is concerned, there is this idea that the priest or minister knows better than you, that the priest has a better connection with God. It is not true.

People have gone from something they consider to be old fashioned in religion, and transferred those ideas to the one that the Ascended Masters are the new gods. The Ascended Masters, of course, at the end of the day, do not deny that they are gods, but they remind you that you are also gods. This is really important to understand.

I hear all kinds of stories in my life, during my travels. I do this kind of work continuously all over the planet. People say to me: "The Ascended Masters told me to do this, and this, and this. I didn't want to do it, but anyway I did it, and things that have happened to me since I don't particularly like." My reply is: "Why did you do it then, if you didn't want to?" The reply to that is again: "Well, the Ascended Masters told me to." My reply to that is really just a few simple words: "So what? Did you learn nothing about standing in your own power? Did you not listen to a word that was spoken in any workshop you attended about standing in your own power and being your own person?"

I find totally amazing that people are willing to give their power away to something outside of themselves in such a way. To me, yes, I have a constant connection with these energies and these beings, and sometimes I may even ask them for some advice, because they are my friends. But if I don't particularly like the advice they give me, I just say: "Thank you very much, but I'm not going do that."

It is most important to understand that you must not give your power away to anything outside of yourself, because as part of the creation of Mother/Father God, you have the perfection of creation in your seed blueprint, and any dis-ease that you suffer is created by not allowing that blueprint of perfection to manifest though you. There is nothing else. The reason why we suffer from dis-ease is because of the illusion of separation and our continuous attempts to deny our true selves. That is the cause of all the physical dis-eases.

When we work with the cosmic properties of gems, of flowers, with the life force of any substance, that life force interacts with our life force to bring us back into harmony and balance. The reason why we created the gemstones, flowers, trees, etc. was to bring these cosmic energies of the knowledge of wholeness in harmony and balance into our earthly context. Of course we, in our physical bodies, are also part of that manifestation of wholeness. It is only through the creation and the interaction with the illusion of duality and separateness that we do not remain whole. Remember this and don't give your power away.

Yes, sometimes they [the Ascended Masters] may have more experience in certain fields than you have, so they can help you through their experience, but they don't know everything. Also, don't get hooked up, or don't get obsessed by the Ascended Masters, because in fact there are billions and billions of other energies of other beings in creation throughout multi-dimensional realities that also have many skills. Many of them have also taken their ascension. It is necessary to understand that when a being has just taken their ascension, and has a degree of multi-dimensional realities, he is still working on the realization of his perfection. Don't work with the illusion that if you have taken your ascension there is nothing else to do, except hanging around in multi-dimensional reality and being cool.

In fact, the way creation works naturally is in constant forward movement. You may be surprised to learn that Mother/Father Source is constantly learning. Don't get stuck in the idea that once you've achieved your ascension it is the end of the road, and everything is just to be sitting on clouds and playing harps. There are plenty of things for all to do. Whether this knowledge makes you happy or miserable, I'm not particularly interested, but just never think that you've got to the end of the line. I find this very exciting, that you never get to the end of the line until the end of a round of creation, when there is the true merging with the Mother/Father Source. That's the only time; that is the end of the road. So don't consider that people in other dimensional realities know everything, because that is just part of the illusion.

As I said before, but some of you probably have not heard it, if things continue to go as they are at the moment, with people attempting to give their power away to these beings we know as the Ascended Masters, the Ascended Masters are saying that they are going to withdraw all communication with this dimensional reality. That will stop people from giving their power to them. It will force more and more people to stand in their own power with their own I Am Presence. Never think that you are anything less than Mother/Father God.

If you insist on giving your power away, give your power to your I Am Presence, and allow the glory of your I Am Presence to manifest through your physicality in this dimensional reality; because your I Am Presence is not something separate from yourself. The reason why you are living in this physical body in this moment is that your I Am Presence chose that. A lot of people forget that. Through their interaction with the illusion, they think that they are just their body, but in fact their I Am Presence uses this body to experience in this dimensional reality. Because of the interaction with the collectively created illusion of this dimension, people forget that.

If you insist on giving your power away, I would advise you to work on giving your power away to your I Am Presence. Then your plan for this lifetime can manifest through you in an easy way, and you will find that all the struggles in your life melt away. The only reason why you have struggles in your life is because you are not doing what your I Am Presence brought you here to do. Your I Am Presence is the reason why you are here.

Each and every person came to do certain things, whether it is to teach others great lessons in different ways, or to learn how to stand in your own power in this dimensional reality, or to empower people through love. The reasons for being here are as many as there are people on the planet. Each one has a unique place in the cosmic plan. Even the people you would judge to be bad or evil or whatever, they are all playing their part in the plan.

Do you know what the cosmic plan is? For everybody to realize that they are gods and goddesses, standing in harmony and balance, no judgment. There is no such thing as good or evil. Everything just is, existing in perfection in the moment. Everything happening on and around the earth happens so the people will come to this realization. Mother/Father God doesn't mind how people are brought into this realization. In fact, human beings, if they feel the need, can actually destroy themselves. If they feel the need, they can also destroy the planet. That's not a problem for Mother/Father God. Mother/Father God will just create another race, another planet. No judgment. You destroy and kill as much as you like, until you learn that all there is is Love, to support each and every being, each and every world.

[Here the Representative of the Confederation of Free Worlds comes in.] *You know yourself as the human race. You are familiar with the types of bodies through which you can experience upon the planet. Originally differences were created by heat and cold, but in fact you are not the first humans that were created upon this planet. Where are those humans now? They don't exist upon the planet anymore, because they destroyed themselves. But the spirits that inhabited their bodies, or shall we say to make it easier to understand, the souls that inhabited their bodies, now inhabit your bodies. You can see that even if you destroy yourselves, or destroy your bodies, you don't destroy your true self.*

From the perspective of Mother/Father God, free will was given to this planet along with other planets within your solar system, and through this free will you already made other planets uninhabitable in the way that you understand habitation: Mars and Venus just to speak of two. Through the action of the beings that were also humanoid beings on those planets, it is now impossible to live there in this type of body, for the ecosystem and the atmosphere have been destroyed. And if the ecosystem is destroyed, these biological forms, or physical bodies, cannot exist without water and oxygen. There is no breathable atmosphere. We would remind you that even your investigating scientists at this moment say that they think they have found frozen water on the planet Mars. They already are starting to think that there must have been an atmosphere similar to the atmosphere of Earth there. In their naivety in the past they always said that life would not exist in a place like that. Of course, in the circumstances they see now it would not exist, but in the past it was.

You have the free will to destroy yourself or live in your own power. This is the choice of every individual, and the things that you see happening around you upon the planet are a representation of what happens in your hearts and your conscious minds. These struggles, the need and the hunger for material power, the feelings of need of having power over others and to control others in their actions, these are the reflections of the consciousness of many, the outward manifestation of their inner realities. It is very easy to change the world. Change what happens in your hearts and in your minds, and the world will change with you. This is the choice, and it is yours to take; for every human being, it is the choice to make.

For we, Mother/Father God and the creator gods, have all the time that we need. We have all the time we need because time is an illusion. We are not governed by time. Only humans govern themselves by time. We can wait as long as it takes, but our choice is that you listen to our words and stand in your own power, be steady in your hearts and minds, and you move forward very quickly. Cease the inner struggle, allow the perfection to manifest through you, and the next level of your experience on this planet will start to manifest very quickly.

Would you understand that Mother Earth is a multi-dimensional being like you are? She has a body in every dimensional reality, just as you do, and it is the same for her and her children. When she decides to take her ascension, she just integrates in another dimensional aspect of herself.

You have the choice of making those steps along with her. As said, Mother/Father God is in no hurry, and if you don't wish to make the steps into wholeness and power, that's all right. There is no judgment. We already have other planets prepared for you where you can continue to disempower each other, print your money and build your weapons, control each other through lack of food, through lack of education, materially and spiritually, lack of resources and housing, until such times that you realize that this is not what true life is.

For us, we would see that the most preferable choice is to move into your own power and cease the struggle. Ask yourself: "Is my continual struggle making me happy? Does my continuous denial of my god/goddess-ness help me in standing in my own power? Does it make things easy for me in my life?" We would hope for you, not for us, because we love you exactly as you are without judgment, but we would hope for you that the answer would be: "I want to make changes now."

Of course, the constant human question is, "How?" The answer in totality from Mother/Father God is, "Just do it". Just allow the glory of your I Am Presence to manifest through you. There is no question or argument. At this moment the human race stands upon a crossroad. The more people are standing in their own power at this moment will have a strong effect on what happens to the human race next. Would you prefer the creation of a heavenly situation upon the Earth? When we say a heavenly situation, we don't mean anything religious or Biblical. A heavenly situation is where all are taken care of, supported and loved, and given the situations that they need to learn who and what they are. Or would you prefer another ongoing period of struggle?

There is a choice, but I know, we know, that humans deep within them have knowledge of their god/goddess-ness. It is not only coded in their light bodies, but in their DNA. Deep down everybody longs for this Oneness and this wholeness. Our advice to you is not to long for it, but to do it.

So, my friends, this is a spontaneous channeling. It amuses us because the channel was not prepared, but we have spoken off. It was decided that through the openness of the channel we would take the opportunity to speak. This channel, of course, does stand in his own power and had the choice to say yes or no.

In fact, we are a group of beings that are a collective consciousness. We are not the Ascended Masters, we are a group of multi-dimensional beings from multiple worlds, humanoids, reptilians and insectoids. We belong to a group which is know as the Protectors of the Emerald Covenants of the Free Worlds, and our group, or you can say our organization, is know as the Confederation of Free Worlds.

You might ask: "Is planet Earth a member of the Confederation of Free Worlds?" We would say to you officially, "Not yet". For the simple reason that human beings haven't realized their freedom yet. Or I would rephrase that slightly and say that there are many human beings that still have to realize their freedom.

This day is coming quickly. This is why we are asking each and every one of you to stand in your own power, because then you will achieve freedom. When you stand in your own power, you cannot be coerced by governments, for you are not afraid of governments anymore. The most extreme scenario is that they can destroy your human body. Notice that I didn't say the worst, I said the most extreme, for you can always incarnate again, so it is not really bad, it is just a change of body. As you stand in your power, you are free from the fear of oppression. You become unshakable in the faith that you are pure love, that you are Mother/Father God incarnated in this body. The will of Mother/Father God will manifest through you.

You have choice, humans: spend another few million years in the slavery of the illusion, or be free now. We hope you make the choice of freedom, so we can welcome you with open arms into the Confederation of Free Peoples.

My friends, I have told you who we are, we have told you what we do. We have given you some ideas, some advice and information. Don't give your power away to us; we have all the power in creation. Stand in your own power and be the gods and goddesses that you are, incarnated on Earth. Don't campaign for peace outside of yourself. Make peace with yourself. As your great teacher, your great master Gandhi spoke, "Be the change you want to see upon your earth, and though your change everything changes."

With our love we leave you now. My name is not important. I am just a spokesperson for this group. This channel has agreed that, within the coming one or two years, he will convey some of our messages to you. We will, at some time perhaps, give you some names, but at this time names are not important, and we know the human potential for getting caught up with names. At this time we will only say that you may know me as the spokesperson.

My friends, in the energy of Mother/Father God's perfection and purity, I salute each and every human upon this planet, and we leave you in showers of our love.

REMEMBER YOUR DIVINITY—A spokesperson of the Federation of Free Worlds (channeled by J.A., 2011)

I'm going to allow a being to speak through me. I don't his name. He calls himself a Spokesperson for the Federation of Free Worlds. He's asked to be given a chance to speak to you. So keep your energy fields open, allow the love to pass around and build and build.

Good morning to you. We know that there are beings here that come from everywhere on your planet. So, good morning, citizens of the Universe. Why do I ask permission to speak to you? I feel that you are a group who are willing to open your hearts, to understand on some level what is happening on your planet. How you have as a race often given your power away, to religions and these other conditionings that the channel speaks of. Now you are willing to step beyond this and to manifest a new reality upon your planet.

So, the new reality is manifesting around you. As you go forward with an openness and a willingness to just love yourselves, to see what is happening around you, the new reality is beginning to manifest. Surely most of you, or even all of you, can feel somewhere deep in your consciousness that this new reality is now totally within your reach. Your world as it is now, and the level of consciousness of the masses, and the amount of interference and control and fear in your lives, is not a member of our Confederation of Free Worlds. As we observe you as a race, and we observe the way in which you interact with your planet and with each other, we see that there is still some way to go before you are invited to join this Confederation of Free Worlds. And of course, if it is a confederation of free worlds, it is a confederation of free people, people with no boundaries, people with no concept of nation, town, city, street, alignments to language, philosophy, religion. It means that you have an opportunity to live in a world where all beings are seen to be as important as each other. It does not matter if your service to your world is high technology, or facilitating healing of those who have come out of balance, or making the gardens grow and producing food, or even making the streets of your cities clean. Everyone is equal in the confederation of free people and free worlds. No one is considered to be any more important than the other. Societies function because all ones are equal and all ones are related to with an openness of heart.

So this is what I encourage you to do: to continue to understand on a much deeper and deeper level that you human beings are the creators of reality in your world, and you have within your hearts this energy of love. You could even say you have the power of love in your hearts, and through this power of love you could distinctly change your reality at any time you choose. Now is the time to make a choice. I encourage you to think carefully, to look at yourselves, to enquire within yourselves and to examine the choices that you made previously, examine the choices that assisted in creating the world within which you live now. Please understand that there is no judgment from our point of view, or anyone's point of view, but you are responsible, all of you, for reality. Every one of you have assisted what you are living upon the planet collectively.

So I ask you please, to just consider a few of the words that I have passed to you today. Also take into your heart, and take into your mind also, the understanding that you as individuals are collective creators and individual creators. There is nothing complicated in understanding this, if only you stand back and disassociate yourself from the illusion that you have come to think is real. Many, many beings say, "If I can't see it, or if I cannot feel it, it cannot be real. So the things of which you speak are not real. How can they be, if I cannot see or touch them?" On the other hand, there is information available to you that says dogs can hear things that humans can't; cats can see energy that you cannot see in general with the human eyes. This is totally accepted. And yet the humans still cannot see or hear it in general. So we have a strange situation here in the minds of humans.

So I encourage you to be focused in your hearts, and as well take into account that it is not your place on earth to convince every individual that you come into contact with, to convince them about the existence of expanded energy, expanded knowledge and expanded love. Your place is to integrate this knowledge within yourselves, to integrate the love within your hearts, and actually to live in this freedom of love, to live without fear. Have no fear of stepping forward. Have no fear of change. What will happen is that the others will see you, and they will say, "Who is this being? How do they live like this? How are they so caring? How are they so loving? How are they so supportive and non-judgmental?" And they will come and ask you, "There is something different about you. Can you tell me what and who you are?" This is the way to pass the word.

Also it's well to use the media machine that the controllers have built. You are already utilizing the internet, that was built by the controllers for their own use. The internet gives you the opportunity to share information with others that you have no other contact with, that you would never have contact with. And if you can use the media, it is the same. It gives you an opening to prompt others to opening, opening, opening.

Our vision for you is that you, as the human race, integrate very quickly and understand what life is about, and that you truly integrate that you are the keepers of this planet, you are the guardians of this planet. This planet does not belong to you. Think again. You are the guardians, the keepers. It is for you, to the best of your ability, to preserve this planet, not to make imbalances, not to rape the Mother. The Earth is your mother. She is a living, breathing biophysical being, *although many forget this. So take care of her, and don't judge her. Many are saying, "We have to heal the Earth." This is a judgment. It is an attempt at programming the Mother with the idea that she is a victim of circumstance. She will accept from you any assistance in openness and love. She does not require victim consciousness, programming and sympathy. Through your guardianship and stewardship, you will be able to transfer to her, through your hearts, the energy that she can utilize to make herself whole. So please approach this in a balanced and sensible manner.*

For yourselves, understand that you are the perfection now, that there never was a time when you were not perfect. For you, the true you, is a spark of Source. Your monad, your true self, is a spark of Source, and therefore is constantly living in the energy of divine Love, perfection, harmony and balance, and any other phrases that you would like to use to explain this state of being. The perfection is manifest within you now, within every cell, every molecule, every atom that composes your physical bodies, your multi-dimensional presences, and so on. We just ask you to understand that you ARE perfection, and allow the perfection to shine through you, instead of believing, for some reason or another, or making an excuse, for some reason or another, not to live this perfection. So please look inside and see it. See that guilt, self-judgment, and these other energies that you may project towards yourself as a human, are actually not relevant to anything. They are all part of the illusion that you have chosen to take part in.

So you have the perfection in your heart, in all your being. I encourage you to live it. And every time that you step out of the understanding, or the realization, gently remind yourselves with love, "Hey! I am perfect. I step back into my perfection, and I allow this perfection to radiate from me." That also assists in others the surfacing of the realization of this pure natural state, of the perfection of the Creator.

So my friends, thank you, for giving me some opportunity to be able to communicate with you. Even if you can only remember three or four words of my communication, I would ask you to remember, "I am perfection, always have been. Always will be. And I realize I am now." This would be a very useful thing to remember.

So please open your hearts to another level of openness, which many of you might not even have been able to have a concept of, something you have not lived in before: an intensity of this divine essence of the truth, harmony and essence of Source. Open, open, open. The channel prompted you earlier to make an affirmation. You may, if you wish, make an affirmation now, one that suits you yourself in your own language. In this moment I will seek permission from the channel to activate the vortex just a little more, to assist you in the integration of this knowledge of the divinity that you are, through the openness of heart.

So I will depart the channel, and put the leadership of the energy back into the heart of the channel. I just again would like to pass on to you that our hearts are open for you, and we encourage you to open your hearts, more and more, moment by moment, day by day, week by week, month by month, year by year. And the perfection will manifest itself in your world. May the energy of Creator, the One Source, be with you.

CHAPTER 5

MORE TEACHINGS FROM HARI DAS BABA AND MASTER GERMAIN

MY ASCENSION—J.A.

I remember when I took my ascension, in 1995 or so, when I found myself, *pffft,* enlightened, zoom, gone! At the time, I was working with a group of Andromedans, and sometimes I would go to their spaceships and stay there for a couple of days and hang out.

I said, "Hang on a minute! I never gave anyone permission to take me anywhere! What's happening!" I looked down, and my body wasn't there in 3rd dimensional reality. Then I appear in another dimensional reality, and all my friends are there. When I say my friends, I mean these people we call the Ascended Masters, but that's just a term we use to describe them. They're friends of mine, and friends of yours too.

I said, "Hey guys, what's happening here?"

Kuthumi says (we all have nicknames for each other, and Kuthumi calls me Yogi), he says, "Hey Yogi, you've just ascended."

I say, "What do you mean, ascended!"

And he says, "You have."

"How can I have ascended? Like, I'm not perfect. And for the last few months I've been emotional as hell. I've been kicking, cursing, screaming, and crying all day long!"

And he says, "Yeah, you've been doing some good clearances, Yogi! You've cracked it, man! You've just ascended!"

I said, "Come on, you people, this is some kind of trick. I mean, I know you're my friends and all that, and we play tricks on each other and all, but I'm not really into this one, and I don't believe a word that you're saying."

So finally Kuthumi and the others said in the end, "OK, Yogi, you don't believe any of us, you think that we're having fun at your expense here, so who's the person that you're going to believe, out of all the masters that you work with and interact with and are your friends?"

I said, "Maitreya."

"All right. Call Maitreya." So, Pffft! Maitreya appears.

"Hiya, Yogi, how're you doing?"

I said, "All right, Maitreya. You're the one that I trust the most out of this lot, and I think they're making fun of me. They all told me that I've ascended."

And he said, "You have." Oh, well, now we have to start thinking about things a little bit, and try and work this one out. He said, "Why do you think you couldn't ascend?"

I said, "Well, I'm not a perfect human being, and I've been going thorough all of these emotional clearances and everything."

He said, "You think any of us are perfect?"

I said, "What do you mean, Maitreya?"

He said, "Do you think any of us are perfect?"

I said, "Well, I thought you guys were perfect."

He said, "That's just an illusion, Yogi. OK, we've achieved mastery, we've ascended, we've got mastery over multi-dimensional realities, we can move through many dimensions. We know things that you don't know, or we've integrated things that you haven't yet integrated. But in fact, none of us are perfect. Because if we were perfect, we'd have re-integrated with Mother/Father Source. So we're still working on our shit, man."

I said, "Ah, Maitreya, now I'm starting to understand."

He said, "You think that when I look into my mind, metaphorically speaking, that I can't find things in my emotional body that I haven't come to terms with, things I'm still working on?"

I said, "Well, Maitreya, I thought you would have, I mean you were the Buddha so many times on Earth, we all thought that you'd achieved enlightenment, and that you were perfect in every way."

But of course, we are all perfect in every way, in our entirety. It's just that, through the illusion of separation, or duality through separation, that we think that we aren't perfect. This is how we continually disempower ourselves, by saying we have to protect ourselves, by always looking for somebody else's opinion of how good we are, and by looking continuously for guidance. I hate this word "guides." I don't like this word because, actually, it implies you give your power away. It implies that they know better than you. And they don't. They can help you, but they don't know better than you, better than your I Am Presence, what your life's path is, and where you should turn right or left. So this word "guides" I never use. I would rather use the word "helpers", because they can be very helpful to us. But this word "guides" also is another scam to make you feel that you have to give your power away all over again.

I remember when I was working in a spiritualist church many years ago, they'd always say, "Well, your guides say this." And I'd say, "Well tell them to go and guide themselves. If they've got any information which can be useful to my life's path, I'm willing to listen, but I'm not going to do whatever they say."

I see this so much in my work. I talk to people and they say, "The Ascended Masters told me I had to sell all my possessions and go sit on top of a mountain."

"Well, are you happy about that?"

"Well, no."

"Well, why'd you do it then?!"

"Because the Ascended Masters told me to."

"What? So you did it?!"

You've got to understand that the Ascended Masters are also a bunch of opportunists. Their focus in their life streams is the empowerment of human beings, and the bringing of complete harmony and balance to Mother Earth, in association with Mother Earth's will. So if they can get you to do anything, they will. But you don't have to do anything that the Ascended Masters tell you, you don't have to do anything that your guides tell you to, and you're not dead if you don't. I mean, people are just desperate to give their power away in this world, because of the way that we have been disempowered.

The Ascended Masters are always saying, "Hey Das, do this will you? Hey Das, do that will you?" If I tried to do even one tenth of what the Ascended Masters tell me to, I'd be a hundred times crazier than I already am. I've got many projects that I'm already working on, but others of them think, "Oh yeah, Das, he's always keen. Ah, Das, can you just do this?" I think that's another reason I was given the name change from Servant ("Das") to Baba. "Hey servant, can you do this?" Even by giving me the name Hari Das, servant of God, by giving me the name "das", servant, they actually kept me in servant mentality. And people reinforced that all the time, thousands of people all over the earth, who called me "Das" for short: "Hey servant, how are you? Hey servant, can you make me a cup of tea? Hey servant, can you enlighten me? Hey servant, can you heal me? Hey servant, can you heal the planet?" and the rest of it.

I know the reason why I was given a new name. Germain said to me, "No longer will you be a servant. You take the next step in your life, and you step into your mastery on another level." So when people say, "What do you think of getting a new name?" I say, "Hey, I've got a promotion, eh? I've been promoted from servant to master!" It's another level of me understanding personally. The way I share with you in my empowerment of you is my personal experiences, mostly. It didn't come from books. It's personal experience, and from my Upstairs Crew.

Recently someone forwarded to the New Paradigm MDT™ e-list, "Let's give up free will and do God's will." I thought that was really beautiful. That is the middle path, isn't it? It's not giving your power away, and it's not exercising your free will to such an extent that you're rebellious. Let's do Mother/Father God's will, and Mother/Father God's will is the empowerment of all beings, in every dimensional reality, human, reptilian, and insectoid. It's the remembrance of the perfection, and the remembrance of the mastery in perfection. It's the remembrance of the beauty, and the remembrance of the love; the remembrance of your male and female aspect in harmony. That's really what we should have in focus.

All this thing about protection and always checking in with agencies outside yourself before you do anything or make a decision or whatever is just totally in the human psyche through the conditioning of disempowerment. Let's get out of it. We don't need it. We can create whatever we need on this planet. Through our own disempowerment, we've created what we see around us, the so-called state of the world as it stands. We've created it. It's come to the stage now that our co-creations as humans are showing us that we don't need this. We don't want this on our planet. I don't want any of what's going on to be happening on my planet. All this strife, struggle, hunger, these struggles for power, for money, struggles for power over the people through systems of medicine that disempower rather than empower, education systems that totally disempower rather than empower—I don't want that on my planet anymore. When I say my planet, I don't think that I own it or anything, but I live here. It's my home at the moment. I came here voluntarily and made it my home. I wasn't forced here for any reason. So when I say it's my planet, I mean it's my home, and I don't want this on my planet, and I'm not going to have it. So I'm going to change it.

What I'm saying to everybody now is, shall we co-create something different with our love, and our harmony and balance, by standing in our own power? Let's not give our power away to anything. Let's stand in our power, be ourselves in our perfection as Mother/Father God in our love. It's as simple as that.

ABOUT ASCENSION—J.A. (Ascension Workshop, 2011)

We'd like to bust some of the myths around ascension. There's so much rubbish around. People don't really understand what the whole process is about. Ascension is not an escape route from planet earth. Ultimately what I've learned since I took my last level of ascension, in 1996, is that we have to get here really as human beings, not hanging about in other realities. At one time I used to be a total space case; people would say, "This guy's really cool, so spiritual." But actually we were just hanging around between realities and not really here in any reality.

Be here now, as a human being, or you can't ascend. Actually, you are spiritual beings having a human experience. You're not lowly humans struggling to have a spiritual experience. It's not like that. Turns the idea of having to struggle to be spiritual on it's head. You have to be Real--a real human being.

Understand what being human is about. When we get grounded into a human body, we have to understand how our insane ego tries to rule us, how we respond to emotional programming, religious programming, sociological programming and so on. All these programs actually in many ways prevent us from having an actual human experience. So you just have to know that, "Yes, I do have an emotional body. OK, I need to get it into harmony and balance, but if I have to do that, it's all right. If I have to live adventures which bring me into understanding, it's all right." It's not a question of judging yourself for not understanding that you are already perfect, NOW. It's all a journey, step by step by step. It's much simpler than we thought. All we have to do is live and accept that we are human beings and we do face challenges, and embrace them with love, and OWN everything. Don't blame things on others. When we experience imbalance, just remember we create it ourselves, so own it. OK, I understand it, I created it, I own it, I love it, I let it go. What can be simpler?

More or less everybody on planet earth, whether or not they're into this search for expanded awareness, or expanded consciousness if you want to call it that, have taken at least 3 or 4 or 5 levels of ascension already. So then you ask yourself, "What am I doing here, if I've already ascended before?" You just chose descension for a change! Remember? You're spiritual beings here having another human experience, and to go on to the next levels.

How many levels of ascension are there? To bring it to human understanding, once you achieve your 12th level of ascension you become Source yourself. This changes the ideas of humans about themselves. Humans believe that Source is the be-all and end-all of everything. But ultimately, you as human beings, everybody on planet earth, after 12th level you become Source yourself and can create your own universe, and the beings that populate it.

This is rather different than the idea that we'll ascend to the 5th dimension and hang out. How boring would that be? Just hanging out in the 5th dimension for all eternity. It's just another step along the way.

Also we have this idea, from working with the so-called Ascended Masters—actually I prefer the term Multidimensional Masters. There are hundreds of thousands of them, but we're most familiar with some who have lived on planet earth. Multidimensional Masters come from all over the universe, in all types, insectoids, reptilians, humanoid, or mixtures. We're not in general interacting with any but the ones who have had lives on earth. Do you think that Quan Yin, or Mother Mary, are just hanging around in the 5th Dimension for thousands of years? It isn't like that. They're not hanging around in the form that they were in their last lifetimes. We don't just ascend to the 5th dimension and just stay there forever.

You can either individually ascend, have a planetary ascension, or a universal ascension. On this planet right now we are going through a level of ascension. The vibrations are changing. Individual ascension is possible, but actually when we have a planetary ascension, everybody will go anyway.

So what about the people who don't want to go? What about free will? Ultimately we have created another 3D planet for them. They can incarnate again to carry on the control systems, create money, build weapons, fight each other until such times as they are ready to move. It's all free will and a journey.

What the project is now is to assist people in understanding these things, and to pass on energies which assist people in activating their energy systems, to be ready for the next piece of personal ascension. So this is what we're going to do, with meditations and such.

Another big misconception is that you have to be very serious about it all. You can laugh your way to enlightenment. You don't have to be so serious. We have to learn to integrate the joy. You have dormant information in your DNA. Actually a large percentage of the codes that you need, that are required [for ascension], you already have, but they're lying dormant, the right buttons haven't been pressed yet to activate them. All in good time, as each one is ready.

Lots of people think that to ascend you have to be holy or something. It's not true. It's nothing to do with holiness. In fact, holiness has nothing to do with any of this. Holiness is self-repression and living in the expectations that others have of holiness. That's why when people say, "How can you smoke and be holy, Baba?" I say, "No problem. I'm not holy. Next question." I used to be very spiritual, but I'm not at all now. I managed to kick the habit. I'm a rehabilitated spiritual person.

So as I said, it's all to do with light. Everyone thinks that Jesus ascended. He never did. The story makes people think that heaven's up there and all. He didn't ascend. It was activation of his sacred geometry to merkaba speed, and then he disappeared into another reality. Melchizedek, Elijah, and Enoch activated his sacred geometry and pfft! Where is he? Gone. So they came up with the story that he ascended into Heaven. Of course there is such a place as Heaven, but it's an illusory place in time and space, in the 4th dimensional reality. There's several different versions of Heaven of course—all in the upper 4th dimension. With true ascension we go beyond all that, out of illusion into reality.

THE MELCHIZEDEK PRIESTHOOD:
Breaking Down Established Thought Patterns—J.A.

The Alpha and Omega Order of Melchizedek is the order of Light, of Love. It's as well to understand that everything has it's dark or shadow side, so there's also a dark Melchizedek order, and they're doing very good work, pushing people's buttons, getting them into the light. But the Alpha and Omega Order of Melchizedek is actually hundreds of millions of members of the Order on the planet right now, often known as the Melchizedek Priesthood.

What happens is, when it's time for a planet to start moving on, when it's time for the people of a planet to start moving on, many, many of the Melchizedek priests and priestesses start incarnating. And they're the troublemakers. Or they're seen by established philosophical schools as troublemakers, because they just break everything up. "We ain't takin' that shit no more, 'this is how it's done'. We've got better ways of doing that." That is what brings the walls down.

Established philosophical schools all operate within very, very definable parameters, and if you go outside those parameters, they'll say to you, "Boy you've got no chance, you've stepped outside the confines of this philosophy." And when I say stepped outside the confines of this philosophy, truly those words echo in the mind: all the times when you've actually done something which sort of winds things up, gets other people going, even just down to small things. For instance, what have we as the New Paradigm MDT family done to the Reiki work?! Shook it to its very foundations, especially in some of the European countries; it's just come tumbling down around their ears.

There's so many of them. Take the Netherlands, Holland, over 16 million people living in a hole in the North Sea. That's basically what Holland is, a hole in the North Sea. There's probably not more than 200-300 square miles of the Netherlands that's above sea level. I always figured they're reincarnated Atlanteans, waiting for the waves to come in again. It's a really crazy, lovable country. In 1998, the Reiki Alliance in Holland actually called up the Center in Tilburg, and asked them, or begged them, not to host any more of our workshops. They said, "This man is ruining our livelihood. This man is breaking down the whole system, and we don't like it." So now they can't charge 30,000 Guilders (3,000 pounds English) to become a Reiki Master. The Reiki Alliance is still charging $10,000 for Master attunements in the United States of America. Actually there are people in the United States who have parted with over $25,000 and still not had a [Reiki] Master's certificate at the end of it. So I've enjoyed doing that in Britain and Europe, and perhaps we're on our way to doing it in the US as well. Even in India they were charging 10,000 Sterling for Master attunements. In India!!! Your average person there hasn't got 10 rupees, never mind 10,000 Sterling. It's incredible. In the [New Paradigm MDT] family now we probably have, the latest update I have, which is probably a year ago [1999], is that there are 5500 activated to the Shamballa energies in the Madras area alone. One lady from Belgium, who has great connections there, gave her guru four level attunements; and her guru is just giving everybody attunements, all comers. Free of charge. If that was 18 months ago, how many are there now?! Everything's starting to break down there. We're going to achieve that in the US as well, so that when someone quotes $10,000, people are just going to break out laughing, "How much?! Heh, heh, heh." So this is just one thing that the Order of Melchizedek has done.

We're also breaking down other established thought patterns as well, like the bastions of New Age fundamentalism. My thing is just to break down all those, because New Age fundamentalism is alive and well on planet earth. You see, some of the Christian fundamentalists, and Jewish fundamentalists, and Islamic fundamentalists have just seen the New Age as something they can bring their fundamentalism into. So you must have all come across it. "What, you eat meat? You drink? You drink alcohol?" Somebody once said to me in a workshop, "How can you drink beer and channel?" I said, "It's dead easy, but you have to take the bottle away from your mouth first." It's the same as the food thing. This isn't a criticism of those who have vegetarian diets, but I would like to point out to you, each and every one of you, that there is only a limited number of people on earth who can actually survive in a healthy way on a vegetarian diet. The reason is that we have different blood groups in human bodies, and different blood groups need different food. Different blood groups actually came here from different star systems. Some can survive very well on vegetables, and others just can't at all. So what is actually being said to you here, and maybe it'll be useful information for you or maybe it'll send you into processing, who cares, is that if you feel like eating meat, do it! I hear so many vegetarians say, "God, I've really been craving meat for the last two years!" Well, why haven't you been eating it, if you've been craving it? Because your body's telling you, "I need meat!"

I myself was a vegetarian fundamentalist for over 25 years. I was so fussy I wouldn't eat in restaurants when I was traveling, even in India. The only place you'll get pure vegetarian food in India is if the restaurant says it's vegetarian. I wouldn't even eat food if I didn't know how it was prepared, that's how fundamental I was. My health was never very good during that period, and I never had a lot of energy. I must have had pneumonia 3 times, I had TB, and I was always down with something or another, listless, pale and all the rest of it, just no energy whatsoever. About five or six years ago [mid '90's] I was visiting these people in the bottom part of England, and they presented me with an English Sunday dinner: roast beef, Yorkshire pudding, crucified vegetables. Do you know why the English were great empire builders? Because they sent people out looking for decent food. Anyway, they had meat, gravy and everything else, and set it on the table in front of me. They were so pleased to have me go and see them, and they were really treating me with so much respect and everything else. I sat there and looked at it, and I thought, "Well what're you going to do now then? Are you going to tell them, "I don't want this, I'm a vegetarian?!"

And it flashed into my mind, a story about a hero of mine, somebody that I really, really respect. He's passed over now, long since, but he's called Swami Vivekananda. He was a great devotee of a man called Ramakrishna, and Ramakrishna was an Indian whose thing was to integrate western and Indian spirituality, Christianity and Hinduism. The system of philosophy that he taught is actually known as Vedanta. Anyway, Swami Vivekananda was a great person. He came to the USA in 1945, to a world religious conference in Chicago. It was the first time that a Hindu had ever spoken at one of these world conferences. He told this story in his memoirs. An American couple asked him to dinner, and they gave him roast beef. Well, he's a Hindu, and cows are holy. So he was sitting there eating the roast beef, saying," This is really nice, what's this?" He'd never tasted it in his life before. They said, "It's beef." And he said, "What's that?" And they said, "It comes from cows." Whoops. He said that his immediate reaction was to run away from the table and be sick. And he said, then "some kind of sanity came to me. And I realized that these people had given me their hospitality, that they really liked me, and they'd gone out of their way to give me this food. So I ate the food."

So that's what came into my mind as I sat there, Swami Vivekananda in my head saying, "Remember the story about Chicago?" And I said, "Yeah." So I ate the food. Later in the night I was laying on my bed, and I was processing. I was thinking, "Shit, Das, you're going backwards! God! Why did you do that (etcetera)." And then there was a flash of light, and Germain was standing there, not an unusual occurrence. So he went, "What's the matter with you then, my brother?"

"Aw man, I'm freaking out. I've been eating meat and all that, and it's really terrible. What a terrible day it's been, slipping away, slipping away to the darkness, eating cows!" And all the rest of it.

He said, "So you think you're qualified to judge the level of consciousness of the beings on planet Earth?"

I said, "What do you mean?"

He said, "Don't you realize that everything is life? Vegetables are alive. You've been eating vegetables. Are you saying that they have a lower level of consciousness than animals? Do you think you're qualified to judge this?"

Then I thought, "I'm getting a working over now for sure!" He said, "Everybody's got habits on planet Earth, and it's about time you got over this vegetarian habit of yours." So then he went on to point out to me about different blood groups needing different food. He said, "Now and in the coming years you won't be able to live on a vegetarian diet. You've managed to get by with it so far, but you're going to be doing so much traveling and so much work that you would just lose your body in no time if you try to keep this up. So I suggest that you actually kick the habit."

I said, "You reckon it's a habit then, Germain?"

He said, "Yeah, it's just the same as the other habits that human beings have. Which leg do you put in your trousers first every morning?"

I said, "Uh, I think it's the right one."

He said, "Well, that's a habit. Why don't you try putting the left one in, for a change now and again. That will help you to break the habit. Which arm do you first put in your shirt, when you put it on? Change it. Which shoe do you put on first? Change the habit. You're all full of habits, you humans. You should start to understand that."

The rest of it goes into a joke, really, because after that, I said to him, "Well, OK Germain, I totally understand what you're saying."

So the next day when I left there, I went to Burger King and ordered a double whopper with cheese and bacon. And since then, I haven't looked back.

So that's how I broke my vegetarian habit. But this fundamentalism is really alive and well in this New Age movement, which we kind of loosely belong to, New Age spirituality or whatever you call it. So, learn to have FUN before DA MENTAL. If you learn to have fun before the mental, everything works easier. If your body asks for meat, just give it meat, don't freak out about it. If your body doesn't ask for meat, well then, don't eat it. You aren't being told that you won't get anywhere if you eat meat or don't eat meat. You've just been given useful information that may help you to run your body, to be healthy.

It's the same as the people who think that alcohol is detrimental to spiritual life, or whatever. Sometimes your body might say, "A good slug of Bourbon would be cool!" Go for a good slug of Bourbon! Or a bottle of wine. Whatever you need. Just do it. Whatever you need in your life, just do it. Don't say, "Well, I can't do this, because I am— whatever." Don't actually repress yourselves, because if you keep the lid on a boiling pot, what happens in the end is that something explodes. And the explosions are much harder to deal with than going with the flow. So that's Germain's bit of wisdom for you on fundamentalism.

There's not actually that many people who've been able to live with the Melchizedek consciousness at this time, in this civilization. But the directives from the Central Sun, from my I AM Presence, is to start linking people with this consciousness, because what it actually does is to help you hold the higher vibrations. In other words, you don't get so easily bogged down. Also, I think that being linked with the Melchizedek consciousness makes it easier for this higher vibration to come through you, helps with the channeling process, and other things as well.

So again you can do it or not do it. If you feel it's appropriate to you, say you accept it, and if you don't, say you don't accept it. It's as simple as that. You might ask your I AM Presence. Everybody will go through processes, eventually, or the workshop wouldn't work! It's simple. What it all involves is changes in consciousness, making adjustments in your thought patterns and everything.

ON CHANNELING—J.A.

The first rule of channeling is "open mouth". People make all kinds of excuses not to channel. They make all kinds of judgments about the channelers. A number of years ago I was double-checking some channeling with Ashtar, and Ashtar said to me, "There's one thing you have to learn, Das, there's not a perfect channeler in the whole of Creation. Channeling comes through your brain, through your mind. You're also grounding the energy through your body. So it's also affected by your emotional body." What it showed me was, if there aren't any perfect channels, then that's all right. It just shows you that you must be discerning. Some people really try to give their power away to channelers. There's people that won't go to the restroom unless they consult a channeler. They won't turn a light on. That kind of thing is giving your power away.

There was a time in my life when I used to do a lot of personal sessions with people. I'd go do a workshop and then spend a couple of days doing personal sessions. Then when I actually passed through that town or city or country again, maybe the same people, or some of the same people, would come to me for personal sessions. It was extremely lucrative. But what I realized was, people would listen to the tapes over and over again. There's one thing about prophecy you should know. I never make prophecies, because these days things change so fast that prophecy is only relevant to the moment in which you make it. When you do a reading for someone, that's a kind of prophecy. You can read the Akashic Records, information banks. Me, personally, I keep a block on my records. If you don't do this, anyone can access them. Just say, "From this moment on my Akashic Records are sealed; no one can access them without my permission." There are really nosy people about.

Prophecy is only relevant in the moment you make it. More and more that is true, in this rapidly changing reality that we live in. A lot of people look back now at the prophecies of Nostradamus and say, "Such and such happened, it's in the prophecies". If you ask ten people, each has a different interpretation of what he said. It isn't relevant anymore. He made those prophecies hundreds of years ago. If things had stayed the way they were when he made those prophecies, they would be relevant now, but because of the earth's changing reality it isn't true. So that's the reason I realized that prophecy is only for the moment. And there are people desperate to give their power away. One thing I really love doing in life is empowering people, not disempowering them.

People try to give their power away to channelers, or they try to give their power away to the energies that the channelers channel. I reckon the easiest beings to channel in this age are the Ascended Masters. What they are telling us is, that if people try to give their power away to them, all channeling will be withdrawn. They will withdraw. What that will do is to force human beings to actually connect with their own I AM Presence for guidance, instead of giving their power away to outside agents.

Nevertheless, being able to channel is quite useful. The Multi-Dimensional Masters, or the Lords and Ladies of Shamballa, whatever you'd like to call them, have a terrific amount of information to give us. Many of them are actually terrestrial beings; they lived on Earth until their ascension. So they can share with us what they went through in the process. They can also loosely make prophecies. Really, the only prophecy I make nowadays is that in 2025 things will be different, and if they aren't, you will have forgotten I ever said it.

How do we channel? Through our channel. When you did this work early on, you were given a symbol called the *antahkarana*. It's' an ancient symbol that isn't actually New Paradigm MDT at all, but Lemurian. This is the name of our channel. If you dig a ditch and run water through it, you can say that's a water channel. So you bring the energy in through your antahkarana channel. Those who do this are called channelers, and the act of doing it is called channeling. The information comes in through your antahkarana. Your antahkarana is also known as your Rainbow Bridge. In the American Indian tradition, some people were given the name Rainbow Warriors. The reason some were given the name Rainbow Warriors, some tribes were called Rainbow Tribes, was because they had their antahkaranas, their Rainbow Bridges, activated totally. They were in connection with All-That-Is. If you see a person who has their antahkarana activated, you can actually see [etherically] these rainbow colors, going onwards and upwards. That's why it's also known as the Rainbow Bridge.

This antahkarana is actually very easy to activate. When you activate your antahkarana, you will be able to channel energy, which you can convert to information. Channelers do vary, and channelers vary in their brain capacity. That isn't any kind of judgment, but some people have brains that handle technical details easily. So they're the people who have technical information channeled through them, because they're the ones who can sort it out in their brain. There isn't any point in giving technical information to a person like me, whose brain does not work with extreme technical things. I can operate a computer, figure out how electronic things work without reading the book, mostly, but if you're getting new technical information through, you need someone who has a technical brain, to be able to decipher that. And if you've got someone like me who is open enough to bring the Love through, and information on how to integrate love, or how to activate the channel process or whatever, then I'm an ideal person to bring that information through. So everybody won't be getting the same kind of stuff.

I find the channeling process very, very easy. It might be the computer syndrome all over again, but I do find it very difficult, often, to understand why people aren't just doing it. After all, you can walk, you can talk, you know how to eat, and all these other things, but you deny yourselves that gift, that gift of channeling. And you deny yourself for all kinds of reasons. You deny it because you may not feel "good enough", a lack of self worth. You deny it because you think that the Multi-Dimensional Masters, the Lords and Ladies of Shamballa or whatever you want to call them, are actually better than you are, just because they've ascended. It's kind of that same religious thing all over again, such as, "The priests are better than us, so we have to give our power away to them." Or, "I can't be a priest! They have to intercede with God on my behalf." Very, very deep conditioning, whether it's through Christianity, Buddhism, Hinduism, Judaism, Islam, whatever. Very deep-seated conditioning. So the first thing that you have to integrate into your own minds is that you are a great channeler this minute, you are a great channeler this second, each and every one. All you have to do is to get on with it, and don't deny it.

We make jokes about channeling, "Where did it come from? Was that me?" "Was that message from God? Ah no, I was talking to myself. Shit!" "Oh, I have a message from God. Why would God be talking to me?" God would be talking to me, or to you, because you *are* God and Goddess. So why wouldn't God/Goddess talk to you? Why wouldn't the Ascended Masters talk to you? After all, they've achieved their mastery. That's it. They're not in charge or anything. People think, "Oh, Masters. They're in charge of everything." They're not in charge of anything except themselves. The same as every other Master should be in charge of themselves, in other words integrating their Mastery. Other than that, they're in charge of nothing. So there isn't any of the energy of the stationmaster, the postmaster, the schoolmaster, or any other masters you've come across in your life, that tried to impress you or force you into doing things you didn't want to do. The Ascended Masters don't do things like that.

The term Ascended Master (Germain likes this one) merely implies that they've achieved Mastery in such a way that they can move inter-dimensionally without going through the process that human beings call "death". That's what they've integrated. Mastery on that level. So there isn't any point in trying to give your power away to them. They don't want it. They don't want followers, either. All they want is to work with you, on an equal basis, person to person, energy to energy, Master to Master, created being to created being. Nothing else. And that's what I really like about it. Any energy that comes to you and says, "I am an Ascended Master, you WILL DO THIS" [Das makes a familiar gesture with his finger] is the reply. When they say, "You will do this!" it's control. True Masters aren't into control, they're into empowerment. I'll say that again. We're not into control, we're into empowerment. They may make suggestions that can make your life easier, that will help you along the path a little bit, but they never say, "You HAVE to do this." And they never say things like, "If you don't do this, you'll never make it." Because as many individuals as there are in the whole creation, there's an individual path for each one. That's why religion doesn't work, in the way that it's taught. Understand that when things get very, very organized, it all turns into a control system as well.

I love this joke. The devil was walking along one day on earth with his right-hand man. They're just strolling along. They see a man walking along in front of them. The man bends down and picks something up. He says, "Wow, a fragment of the Truth!" The right-hand man turns to the devil and says, "Look, Master, he's just discovered a fragment of the Truth!" And the devil said, "Don't worry about it. I'll arrange to get it organized." That is the bottom line in all this tightly organized stuff. It becomes a control system. So these Masters, these beings who have achieved mastery of multi-dimensionality, are never going to try and control you. It isn't the way things work. Empowerment through freedom is the way it goes.

ON DODGY CHANNELING—J.A.

There can be a reasonable amount of delusion [in some channeling] because of this need to be important, this need to be recognized, this insecurity, and people not understanding their place in creation. Some people will listen to any kind of channeling, and they'll bring through any kind of channeling. Also as well, there is no channeler in the whole of creation that has 100% pure information. Sananda told me this years ago. It comes through the brain and it's processed, so there will be an aspect of your character mingled with it. So I asked him the best way to check out how straight a channeling is. He told me that the rules are very simple. If there's any fear-based information about destruction of individuals or the planet, ignore it. You may be privy to information that you can pass on to groups you work with, to alert them to certain possibilities, but don't bother about these widely-circulated predictions of mass destruction. Also watch out for those channelings that tell you how beautiful you are, how wonderful you are, "we love you, don't worry, we'll fix everything up, just give your power away to us and we'll deal with the lot." That's dodgy channeling as well. "And don't forget to send all your cash."

I'm very familiar with the energies that I channel. No one can duplicate the true essence of Germain, for instance. I do have them try it, mind you! But I know that it isn't Germain. So I just tell them, "I'm surprised you're trying to pull this one again! Bug off!" But that's come to me through experience. I've been told a few times that I'm not channeling Germain; it's just from my ego. Well, I'm extremely confident in what I do, and that can be construed as coming from ego, because I don't have any aspect of my character that says that I can't do this. I know that I can do it. So it's like anyone else who's extremely competent. When you get the master craftsman, he's not saying, "I can't carve this stone," or "I can't build" or whatever. He knows he can do it. So that's where I'm coming from. Becoming confident in the way that you channel is the way to keep your channeling as focused as possible.

There are all kinds of ways people say you can check things, but I consider that's giving your power away. If you have the focus in your heart, in love, then there's absolutely no dodgy energies that can come through you. It's as simple as that. It's only when you have some aspect of fear, or denial, that you're open for the tricksters.

ASCENSION, REINCARNATION, WHAT'S HAPPENING NOW, & THE DIVINE PLAN—J.A.

I know one thing; I'm not coming back to this planet again. This is my 123rd visit to this planet, and by the time I leave this time, there won't be any need for me to come back here again. So for me personally, I don't think this applies.

But for many people, I think that as you quit this dimensional reality, whether you do that through physical ascension or through actually leaving your body, I don't really see that one method is better than another. I mean, although some people feel that full body ascension is more glamorous than dropping dead, that's judgment, you know. Dropping dead is just changing consciousness.

Humans are not really attracted to dropping dead. They've got this thing, "I need my body!" They don't understand that, actually, being born is a much more difficult process than dying. But it's just the way things are. You know, "I don't want to leave my collection of crystal skulls behind!" "I've got a lovely car and a nice house and a lot of money or whatever, I don't want to leave it behind. I need my body!" And all that bit.

Depending on which way you choose to actually leave (of course everybody will ultimately), for me I see that you have to really make it to 8th or 9th dimensional reality. So you need to have compatible vibrations with that level of manifestational creation. Because that really just takes away from all the attractions of 3rd dimension, the attractions of the body, the attractions of the things you can do with the body, you know the senses, sight, sound, smell, all that stuff.

I'm incredulous how attracted people are to this planet. People are dying to get here! They take birth after birth after birth after birth, get themselves more and more confused, more and more confused. It seems like it gets harder and harder for them to get out of the illusory aspects of life here. For me, heading out, raising your vibrations, even if you can't make it to Source so to speak, as an individual, set your sights high, and go for it. Just decide, "I don't need that experience anymore."

Of course, a lot of people come here at special times, and this is a special time. That's why there are a lot of special people incarnate on the planet. There's even angels incarnating every day, never been here before. It's incredible, the amount of attraction to what's going on here. It's just such a new thing. Ten years ago we were saying, "We're going to ascend to the 5th dimension." But the expansion of consciousness has been so rapid, and the plan is an open-ended plan. Not only is this earth going to ascend, the whole universe is going to ascend. That's just changed in ten years. And ten years is nothing out of the whole of creation. It might seem a long time if you're hanging out and waiting, it might seem awhile in a human body, but out of infinity it isn't anything. I mean, just in the flick of a finger we've done that, as the human race. Ultimately where we're going, the plan is totally open-ended. Humans have definitely surprised the Creator, Mother/Father God, as his/her own Creation, certainly surprised the other creator gods, the Elohim and the others, and the councils, too. Some of them are standing around with their mouths open. Wow. That lot is really getting it together.

There have been times when we've almost destroyed this planet, and we've almost destroyed each other. In the fullness of Creation, the creator gods never worried about that. I mean, that was great while it lasted, let's do another one now. It's as simple as that. Although everyone's attracted to their bodies, what they forget is that they are an individual spark of consciousness that really hasn't got anything to do with this body. Although consciousness is using this body as a vehicle of expression in this dimensional reality.

The sad part of it is that humans have come to identify themselves as this body, rather than as spirit. You know, although you might feel sad when you take your car out to be scrapped, squashed, because it's served you well, it didn't break down a lot until it had a major trashing, or something like that; that's the way you should view your bodies, too. You know, your bodies are temples of the soul, and as such, you have to look after them, nurture and love them, but you really don't have to bother anything else about it. Understand that you can always have another body. A large percentage of human beings have forgotten that they're just recycled dust. That's what you are. If the consciousness leaves this body, and you leave it lying on the lawn, in not much time at all there wouldn't be much left. It will actually have gone back to the elements, back into Mother Earth. You [in this body] are actually constructed out of enough iron for a 6-inch nail, enough sulfur for a box of matches, and some recycled dust.

You need to integrate this, that you are spirit; you are an individual spark of consciousness that was created by Mother/Father Source. You have all the potential of Mother/Father Source, because you are Mother/Father Source. So you see what all this work is about. All roads lead to Rome, ultimately. There's a million ways of doing it. But the words that have been spoken in the last ten minutes are things that everybody really needs to learn fast. Just understand that we are eternal beings. In this round of creation there wasn't a time when you weren't, and there won't be a time that you aren't. But you won't be in the same human body. And what about before you were humans? There are a lot of you who were other things before you were humans. There are different forms of creation. You could have been reptoid, you could have been insectoid.

Well in fact you have, all of you, just the same as I have. Some of you were silicon based, so you were crystal. I'd like to get you away from your ego-based stuff. And also, this ego-based stuff, "I need to know, I need to know, I need to know." You're already 5th dimensional. That's why we're giving you these activations, to remind you of your multi-dimensionality, to reconnect you to those parallel worlds, multi-cosmic aspects of those worlds. Just reconnect you. And hope that the bells ring, "Yeah, I'm 5th dimensional! What's 5th dimension like?

Yeah! I'm here! In fact I'm living here. I've been living here since I was created! I just forgot that, just got embroiled down here."

On the other hand, however, the only way you can do this whole process of enlightenment is to be fully integrated into all of your bodies. Now, you here on planet earth, this is the densest body you've got. Like I said, recycled dust. You need to ground all these energies into your physical body, and that's why it's necessary for you to be here now. We spent so many years trying to get out of it. Me, I was an expert at getting out of it, whether it was sex, drugs, rock 'n roll, channeling, dancing, whatever. I've got millions of ways of getting out of it. I've spent three quarters of this lifetime looking for ways to get out of it.

One day I realized, "Hey, man. You've got to get *in* it." Once I realized that, everything changed for me. I had had all this access to multi-dimensional realities, and access to the whole of creation. But I didn't have it in relation to this dimensional reality. All I ever wanted was to get out of this dimensional reality. About 20 years ago or so I realized it was time to get here now. But I really had to work at getting here now. I realized I had many, many potentials in many other realities, but I hadn't realized the potentials that I have here. So a part of being here, a part of Mastery, is the art of being here now, and dealing with the present.

That's the great thing about it. Somebody said this morning, "God, I'd die if I had to do a 4-day workshop without any notes." And I said, "I didn't really know what I was going to do until I got here. I knew I was going to give you 13 activations, but after that I didn't know anything. I'm just an ordinary person. I've learned how to stand aside and let my I Am Presence and the others work through me." She said, "Well that makes you not an ordinary person."

But I still insist, I beg to differ on it. I've only learned how to work in that spontaneity since I've learned to *be* here. But by learning to be here, I've also reinforced my connections with the other dimensional realities. I think my next comment was, "God, if I had to go to every workshop with a bundle of notes, I'd have taken up robbing banks by now, instead of workshopping!" Because to me it would be such a boring existence, having to do the same thing over and over and over and over again. Learning to be here now is also like learning how to work with the magic. Learning how to work with the magic is really simple. The magic works, because in your Mastery you say that it'll work. My guru always told me that if you want to go on the spiritual journey, you have to pick up your foot. Because unless you pick up your foot, you're not going to take a step. So you aren't going anywhere. There's no point standing around saying, "Why aren't I going anywhere? Nothing's happening." Because you haven't picked up your foot. Every journey that you take starts with that first step. Yes! Now we're moving. Yes! I didn't fall over. And another one.

And how do you connect with the energies? You hold out your hand. You don't stand there with your arms folded, "There ain't nothin' out there. Hey you lot!" "Yeah, we know you're down there." "You lot, well, I can't hear anything. I don't feel you." Hold your hand out, "Here I am." Pick your foot up at the same time. "Here I am and here's my hand!" They say, "Yes! Let's go on a journey! Let's go on a trip!" It just happens like that. It's just spontaneity.

What New Paradigm MDT and the energy of Shamballa does is, it empowers people. People do workshops with me, and then they write to me, "Baba, could you tell me how many times I'm supposed to do this?" And I think, "What did I tell them in that workshop?!" I just say, "Get on and do it!" When you stand in your Mastery, it doesn't matter how many times you do this or that. It works! Because you, as a Master, say to anything, "Move," it does! When you say, "OK, you're activated. Pfffffft!" You are! The person is! It's intent. The intent is everything. It's not the ritual.

In the old days, rituals were great. I remember when I was in India, in the temple, I was really holy, I'll tell you. I was so holy that you would not believe. In the mornings I'd be up early, doing all the paraphernalia for the deities. Sometimes I'd make special sweets for Krishna, and all this. So, Haridas the holy. And I'd be chanting, and blessing everybody, eat the occasional sweet. Krishna was always into stealing sweets, so he shouldn't mind. But there's all that ritual, ritual, ritual, and everything had to be done in exact perfection. You had to remember every step of it; otherwise you'd be damned. And I remember one day thinking, "What is all this? Say I do it 50 times instead of 33, what are they going to do about it?! They couldn't care less." *Yes!* Now I'm starting to understand. God doesn't care how many times you do it. It's just a fact that when you say, "Krishna, come to me. Open my heart and come to me." Krishna says, "Sure, yeah!"

So, in the old days we were controlled by ritual, and we still have that memory in our minds, that if you don't get the ritual right it won't work. But by now we should have integrated the fact that we're Masters. Part of Mastery is that when we say energy moves, it does. When you say, "I create", you do. So remember, you're part and parcel of God/Goddess. And how does God/Goddess create? In the beginning was the word, and the word was "OOOOMMMM." The word was God. Simple as that.

So integrate that you are multi-dimensional Masters. You can do anything. You can clear your stuff whenever you like. Or you can hang onto it as long as you like. But when you say, "I let go, and I let God", everything changes. "I let go and I let God. I trust in every moment, the perfection of creation."

I Came to Earth II

One day I decided to see around,
more of the universe that was around,
came to earth, and well, for what it's worth,
I found an amazing place,
full of love, beauty and a smiling face.
Some say, no, it's a hard place,
me I say do not fear,
we have it all on earth my dear,
we just need to remember to share,
then really we are getting there.
On earth things will change
when all the mess is rearranged.
Just remember all hearts are open,
it is a rule unspoken.
OK now love and love,
for you may think gifts are from above,
but no, they come from life on earth,
from happiness and strife and mirth.
Just be your true self, love.
love baba
John Armitage, 2014

ON SANANDA (JESUS)—J.A.

I'm just going to say a bit about Sananda. Someone was asking who he is. We tend to think everybody knows what we consider to be basic. He was Jesus. He was just called Jesus in that lifetime. I mean, he did cause quite a stir during that lifetime, when he was Jesus. People are still talking about it now. It really shows he made an impression on the consciousness of human beings.

He was 30 years old when he started doing his stuff. Previous to that he was clearing his stuff. He'd been studying with various kinds of monks, yogis, magicians, including Tibetans and Druids, Indians, many others. He was very, very well traveled. His uncle was Joseph of Arimathea, who had all the setup necessary for traveling, because he was a commodity trader. He knew about taking caravans to China, he had boats, knew about navigation. Contrary to popular belief, people were sailing around the world long before people nowadays have an inkling that they were. People came to America long, long before Germain came here as Christopher Columbus. There were lots of visitors, as well as the native inhabitants. In fact, there is this story in Iceland that they were here. Also Scots/Celts and Chinese people.

But Jesus got around all over the place when he was young. Mother Mary was his guru, as is every woman the guru for her children. Many women seem to have forgotten, or lost sight of, that fact, not as a judgment but as an observation, that women are the gurus for the future. They are the people who have the most influence on children when they're young. So Mother Mary had taken on the task of being the first guru of Jesus. Then, as time went on, he did his journeys and all the rest of it. I was around at that time; that's where the jokes about Luke come from. Jesus and I were actually quite good friends. I went on a lot of the travels. I was two years older. When we went to

Glastonbury, in what is now the UK, I was 16 and Jesus was 14. They say he was the Son of God. Well, aren't we all? No argument in that. His mission in that life was twofold. He came to teach us about Love without condition, forgiveness, non-judgment and healing.

He became famous for the crucifixion and resurrection, but then of course the church took it and contorted everything and said Jesus died for you, to make you feel guilty. If you can keep people feeling guilty, they're not empowered. So it's just part of this experiment of religion. Really there's nothing wrong with religion, except that it's a bit like the statement I made on a TV show: all religion is actually a bastardization of the truth. Contained in every religious philosophy is the absolute truth, but the way it's put over, and especially translated from other languages, the truth starts to become very well hidden.

Sananda's surname is Kumara. You might have heard of the Kumaras, any of those of you who have studied Hinduism; you might have heard that the Kumaras are the first created sons of Brahma, the Creator. There's Sanat Kumara, the Planetary Logos, and the others, whose names escape me now.

Before Sananda came here, in his Palestinian ministry, he incarnated on Venus. He's not Venusian, but he did incarnate there. And of course, the beings of Venus are very much concerned with Love without conditions. We know that even in our very basic 3D philosophy, it's often said that Venus is the goddess of love. So that's just a bit of the background of Sananda. And what a great being he is. He's just a being full of love, full of compassion for all, for everything and everybody, and he's available for everybody to work with. I used to have a campaign, "Jesus save me from your followers!" I got that one in Bolder, Colorado. What can I say, he's starting to ground his energy in me, and I'm becoming overwhelmed by the magnitude of the love that he brings with him. He's a really great being. So we'll let him tell his own story.

JESUS/SANANDA ON HIS PALESTINIAN
MINISTRY—Channeled by J.A. (Nesvik, Iceland on Easter Sunday, 1999)

I AM Sananda. I AM the being that is known also as Jesus the Christ. This time of year in the calendar of the beings that follow the philosophy known as Christianity is an important time. Many ones celebrate my supposed death on the cross. Mother Mary told you yesterday that my crucifixion was not something that just happened by accident. In fact, the plan had been formulated many thousands of years ago, during a period of history that some of you would know as Atlantis. During that time, I was a king, an Atlantean king. In those days, the kings were also priests and holders of the knowledge and energy. It might surprise you that also during that life I was martyred. I use the word martyred in a very lighthearted way. But I was captured, taken and killed. And guess who was the person that told them where I was hiding. It was the being that you now know as Judas.

Understand, that over many thousands of years, the way was prepared for the crucifixion. The school of philosophy, or the philosophical knowledge of these scenes was incarnated upon the planet. Understand that these scenes originally came from the mystery schools in Egypt. The mystery schools of Egypt were founded by beings who had left Atlantis before the destruction of that continent. When I say the destruction of that continent, it is not 100% true, for at the time of the final destruction, the continent had been split into six islands. Not only do you get a religious lesson to hear, you get a historical lesson, also! The scene, the knowledge of these scenes was founded, was given to them by Melchizedek. Many of you would wonder where the name Melchizedek comes from. Search the Old Testament of what is known as the Christian Bible, and you will find the name Melchizedek mentioned at least 30 times.

The writings left behind by these beings are known as the Melchizedek Dead Sea Scrolls. So, these scrolls have been found and decoded, but the contents are kept a secret. The contents are kept a secret by this organization that is known as the Roman Catholic Church, with headquarters at the Vatican. For if the contents were made public, Christianity and its control system would be finished in a second. For all ones would know the truth about my Palestinian ministry, and would say that the churches were just controllers, and they had lied about many things.

The essence of my Palestinian ministry was healing based on love. I am sure that many of you know that my Palestinian ministry only lasted for a small number of years. You may ask yourselves what I did before that. And of course, if I did not die on the cross, you may ask what I did after that. When the time came for the crucifixion, myself and my inner disciples were gathered. My inner disciples were, of course, the twelve. I had many more disciples than these twelve. Understand that the word disciple means pupil. I taught many, many people the mysteries that I had learned from the Druids in England, from the sadhus in India, from the Tibetans, from the disciples of esoteric Judaism, and others.

Understand that I traveled and studied for many, many years, and studied under many different teachers. My travel was mainly facilitated by Joseph of Arimethea. Joseph traded in metals, so he was therefore used to travel, and had boats at his disposal. Many beings in this time would wonder how he managed to travel so far in those days. Understand that travel was very common, and in fact, beings traveled from Europe to America, from Egypt to America, and even from Egypt to Australia. One of my constant traveling companions was Luke. I share with you that Luke was also this channel through which I now speak [John Armitage].

When we were gathered, my close disciples were afraid, because I had given them information about the plan on my crucifixion. They decided to try and hide me, out of selfishness. They did not want to lose me, because they looked to me as the leader and Master. We were at the Garden of Gethsemane in Jerusalem, and I knew that the Romans would not find us. I gave instructions to Judas, who had again incarnated in that life, to take on the task of telling the Romans, to tell them where I was, so the crucifixion would take place. Many Christians conveniently forget that Judas was instructed to go and tell the Romans about myself. In fact, it is recorded by Luke and Matthew that I did give these instructions.

Understand that many people were crucified in those days. And many, many people survived these crucifixions. It was not the custom to pierce the human body with swords or spears during the crucifixion. Having nails driven through your hands and feet to attach you to a cross was the punishment. You were also tied onto the cross. Many ones were gotten off the cross still alive and many survived the injuries caused by the nails. Obviously some died from shock and infection, etc. We had laid the plans so carefully that the crucifixion was to take place in the afternoon on a Friday. Sundown on Friday is the beginning of the Jewish shabbat, or sabbath. It was against Jewish law for people to be hanging on the crosses in Jerusalem during the sabbath, so we knew I would not have to spend much time hanging there. On the cross I took my 5th initiation. It might make you all joyful to know that you will not have to be nailed on the cross for your 5th initiation!

During the time I was on the cross, an energy mandala was held by the close disciples. Also some energy was held by my mother, by Mary Magdalene, and some other female followers. This energy was held in the form of six-pointed star mandalas. These six-pointed star mandalas bring down pillars of light from the Source.

One thing happened that was not in the plan. Understand that all ones have free will. Because so many people were pushing forward in the crowd, holding their hands out to me and giving me energy, one Roman soldier in particular started to feel bad-tempered. He felt that if he killed me, the crowd would stop pushing forward. I was pierced with a spear under the ribs. Understand that through my studies with the priests, the holy men, and the yogis of many traditions, it was possible for me to slow down my bodily functions. And with the aid of many ascended masters, angels, archangels and celestial beings, I managed to keep a thread of consciousness in the physical body. Joseph of Arimathea had already purchased the cave of what you might know as the tomb. For it was part of the plan that, when I was taken from the cross at the beginning of the Jewish shabbat, I would be taken to the cave and joined by Luke and many others. Many of you will not know that Luke was also a healer. He knew about ointments and crystals. On a physical level it was his task to tend to my wounds so they healed quickly.

When they got me to the cave, the thread of consciousness left my physical body, and what you 3D/4D beings call death had taken place. The ascended and galactic masters, the angels, and the archangels, and some extraterrestrial beings were persuading me that it was possible to again get back into the body. The experience that I had been through was very traumatic, and even though I could keep control of my emotional body and stay focused in the love, I stated that I would use my free will and not come back to the body. If I had not come back into the body, the plan would have never been completed. So the others tried to persuade me even more to integrate my consciousness with the body physical. As I started to integrate with the body, it was like integrating with a cold wet cloth. The temperature was dropping, because the life force had departed. With a big effort from myself and the others I did again integrate with the body.

During this time many of the others, Mary Magdalene and many of the other disciples, had been sent away. Joseph, Luke, Matthew and one *or two others were left. So they moved me away to another safe place and sealed up the cave. It was on a Sunday that the women went back. My body was gone, and everybody thought I had ascended. Only a small number knew what had happened. Of course, this was too much of a secret to keep. When people knew that I was still alive, everybody said that it was a miracle, and the resurrection had taken place.*

Once the news was out that the resurrection had taken place, or what was thought to be the resurrection, it was necessary to move fast. The Jewish elders again pressed the Romans to disperse my disciples and my devotees, and to kill as many of them as possible. Many were smuggled away. Under cover of darkness they traveled to different parts of the world.

As time went on, of course, everybody saw something happen that they considered to be me taking my ascension in public. This took place on a mountain in the center of Israel, that you now know as the Mount Tabor. Many do not know that I did not ascend at that time. The energy that was seen, the white light that was seen going up into the sky accompanied by angels and archangels, was the energy of Maitreya, accompanied by Melchizedek and Elijah. Not many know that it was the energy of Maitreya that I used in my healing work. And many do not realize that it was the words of Maitreya that I spoke in my teachings.

Understand that it was never considered that my presence on earth would lead to a massive control system and the death of millions of people in my name.

I myself traveled to India after the crucifixion. There was much traffic between India and that area that you know as Palestine, or the Middle East, in those days. There was a very well beaten path, which many of you would know as the Silk Road. It was possible for a group of us to disguise ourselves as merchants and camel drivers. And we made the trip to India and onwards into Kashmir. In due time Mary Magdalene joined me there [after staying for a time in what is now southern France]. We settled there and had children, and I taught people about light, love and healing. That physical body is buried in Kashmir. For those of you that might feel you need to prove this, go to Kashmir and you will find a tomb of Isus.

Many of the other disciples and followers went in different directions, and shared their knowledge too. Many ask me, Isus, Jesus, how will people know that we are teachers? My reply to them is the same as my reply to all teachers. Ones will know you by your love, and by your actions.

Some of you may wonder why I did not ascend after the crucifixion. I did not ascend because I had one trait in my character that I needed to get over. The energy of martyrdom was in my consciousness. I had volunteered twice for martyrdom. Because of this, I felt that I needed to work more things out on planet Earth. I did not take my ascension until my next life. In my next life I was known as Apollonius of Tyana. During that life I experienced a lot of persecution also, because I made public many of the ancient mysteries of the Mystery Schools. After my ascension, most of my work, most of the knowledge of my work, was destroyed, so the ordinary people could not study it and become enlightened [and what had survived then was later destroyed in the fire at the Library in Alexandria]. So there I give you some history of the being known as Jesus the Christed one. It was never anticipated that the religious control system would be built around my presence upon the planet. Our plan was to spread unconditional love, non-judgment and light.

So I understand, brothers and sisters of light, that you have had a long weekend. Many changes have taken place within you, energies have been activated. You have been given new knowledge and techniques. I encourage you to use them.

Although many may feel sad by this story, you must understand that it is part of the progress, part of the learning, part of the whole process that the whole of humanity have gone through to bring them to this state now. And understand that even if I had died upon the cross, I would still be around. So, brothers and sisters of Iceland, I give you my blessings and love. I ask you to understand that you are all Christed beings. That within your genetic coding and DNA are the Christ code, and you can very easily achieve what I achieved in my Palestinian ministry. I do not suggest you should aim towards crucifixion, but spread the love and spread the light.

There was one thing that happened in the hours before the crucifixion that almost meant that the crucifixion would not take place. I was the person that had to carry the cross up to the hill. It was very heavy. We had not had any sleep for a few days, and I kept dropping it. And in the end, the Roman soldier shouted at me, "I don't care what your name is, if you drop that cross once more you are out of the procession!" [Joke]

So my friends, blessings to all of you, and Namaste. Remember I did not die on the cross, so do not feel guilty.

NOTE FROM J.A. (3/25/2009) on the above channeling from Sananda: Mary Magdalene did join Jesus in Kashmir for a bit. She had been in France first, and returned there after. Mary's thing was to anchor the energy in or on the European mainland, and attempt to bring the Europeans into Love. Some say Jesus was in France as well, but this is not correct. It is easy to understand how the mistake is made, by looking at the records or history. Sure there was a person called Jesus in France, but it was not the father Jesus, but a son of Mary and Sananda. As it is today, we often call our kids by the same name as us. One of my two sons is called Michael John; I am John Michael. So the records of Jesus in France refer to the son of Sananda and Mary, or one of them.

GIFTS—Master Germain, channeled by J.A.

Every person brings us a gift, whether we are able to see what the gift is, or whether we are open to receive the gift at the time. Everything that happens to us in our lives is a gift. At very high altitudes, trees adjust themselves, so that the wind doesn't blow them over. A tree which is huge at sea level, at 30,000 feet above sea level still grows, but adjusts itself, so that the winds don't blow it, so that the cold doesn't damage it. We can see that the consciousness of the tree is exactly the same, whether it is at sea level or at 30,000 feet above sea level. So we can see each and every one of us like that. When the winds blow strong and cold, well then, we just adjust ourselves, so that the wind blows through us, instead of blowing us over. So I understand that the winds have been blowing cold, and many are at an altitude that they are not used to. It's a question of holding your consciousness, that greatness that is you, that expansive consciousness, that expansive being in creation. Just allow the winds to blow around you and stand steady, stand steady in your love, stand steady in your hearts, stand steady in your minds, stand steady in your light.

I'd like you to understand, each and every one of you, that every situation we are put in helps us to grow. Sometimes in this growth process, as human beings, when we don't understand what the process is, when we don't understand what is happening around us, through our feelings of separation, then it's possible for our conscious minds to start running amok. Again, I don't criticize, I observe and I pass on to you what I observe. When I say it's possible for the conscious mind to run amok, I mean it's possible to go back into fear-generated feelings of separation. For when the conscious mind is not focused, you are like a cork on the open sea, being buffeted by the waves. All it takes to bring yourself back into focus, is to look into your heart, to look into your mind, and to say, "I Am, I Am the Divine, I Am Love, I Am steadfast, for I Am of the Creator, Mother-Father God."

Also I observe, and I have listened to many things that people have said during these past days. I would like you to understand that your divinity is with you on a 24-hour a day basis. You are divine whether you are asleep or you are awake. Many discount the time that they are sleeping. They don't understand that they are totally present. Many don't understand that it could be said that when you are awake, you dream, and when you are asleep you dream. Because of the nature of the mind, ones tend to relate to the waking state as totally real, and to the dream state as an illusion. To understand your divinity, 24 hours a day, understand that tests come your way in waking life and in sleeping life. I would say to you a reminder of what the Aboriginals of Australia say, "Wake up and dream." For it is through grounding our dreams, both in the waking and sleeping state, that we learn to become more solid, more solid in our understanding of our true nature. Wake up and dream, wake up and dream! Spend a moment allowing your minds to wander through the dream. What do I choose to dream and manifest? Do I choose to dream and manifest that I am alone, that I am not of Mother-Father God and therefore not part of the whole of Creation? Do I choose to dream that I am Mother-Father God, and I am the whole of Creation? Allow your minds to wander around this concept. Am I going to believe, or am I going to program myself, that I am not in charge of myself in any situation? For each one is in charge of themselves, and nothing, or nobody, any power, any energy, is, except for you.

We understand that life does not always seem easy. I Germain relate to my lives on Earth, when I was Francis Bacon. It was not easy. I was pressed and pushed in all directions, by the royalty of the country which I lived in, and by the powers that obeyed the wishes of the royalty. There were many times that I felt, "I don't want to be here. I cannot deal with life. Perhaps I would be better if I were not alive in this body."

When I was in the courts of Europe in the French palace at Versailles, many do not realize what my work was. I incarnated there, I grew up, and my task that I had taken upon myself was to avert the bloodshed, the chaos and the mayhem of the French revolution, to bring harmony and peace into that society, without one life being lost. I took my ascension and came back. I worked on my project for nearly 500 earth years. 500 earth years! And I failed. When I say that I failed, I mean that many lives were lost, there was much chaos. Much, much chaos.

When I finally decided to leave, and go to this place known as Transylvania, and set up a place there that held what is known as the Violet Flame, I changed my identity, I changed my name. I founded a house there, founded a family there, Rakoczy. In my castle the violet flame burnt upon the earth. After I felt that I'd done everything I could, I decided again to take my ascension, just decided to move out of this dimensional reality. And what happened? You've heard the legends of vampires from Transylvania. These stories were made around my castle, because nobody understood what the light was that shone from there. As the Violet Flame burnt in the center of my castle, nobody could understand the emanations. So shall we say, the energies that do not have your immediate freedom in their minds, built up a whole story that this was a very dangerous place, that there were beings there that would drink your blood, and turn you into the living dead.

Again, it could be construed that I failed. I could have said, the French revolution was a failure. This place that held the Violet Flame in Europe, my project was a failure. As Francis Bacon I was a failure. I have other lifetimes: I was Noah. Remember? The one with the boat. I can tell you that this boat actually wasn't a boat made of wood. It was a spaceship. I manifested this spaceship. And I took into the safety of this ship some humans and many species of animals from your planet, because I knew there was going to be a disaster. I took the ship away from the planet for a while, and held everybody in safety. I then, in association with a group of beings from the Pleiades, brought the people and animals back, when the earth was safe again.

I could look around now and say, why did I do it? I could judge the Earth and say it is not a safe place. But that would be from my feelings of separation. That would be from feelings of loneliness and unsupportedness. That would be from the feeling that Mother/Father God does not support me. Instead I look at your earth, or I should say, I look at our earth, for I am also part of it; I have been associated with it from the beginnings of time. I worked upon my ascension process, I worked upon my Mastery, after I had taken the descent into illusion, just the same as every other being chose to take the decent into illusion. I worked, I played, I laughed, I cried, I was sad, I was happy, I was angry, I was threatened; everything happened to me, as has happened to you. And in the end, I fully realized the divinity within me.

That didn't make me a saint. Because remember, saints are created by the Catholic church and the Pope. I was never a member of the Catholic church. I was never a preacher. It was from my family line, my family name, in my life in France, that this prefix in my name came into being. So don't think that I was always perfection. Don't think that I was always in my mastery. This is why I support each and every one in their processes, with my love. It is very easy, when you are in the human body, to link with your supposed frailties, the frailties of body. Remember that these bodies are frail. They can be destroyed very easily. You could drop something upon them. You could fall over something. It could be burnt. But I realized my frailty. Not only the frailty of my body, but also the frailty of my mind. I came to understand, through linking with Mother/Father, that that is what I am. And that is why I was given the job, or

I took on the task, I volunteered to be a teacher, to be a figurehead, an energy which people could relate to while they were incarnate upon the planet.

I will say to you, brothers and sisters, that even now sometimes I wonder, even now sometimes I wonder, am I empowering in the way that Mother/Father God desires? And every time I wonder, Mother/Father God comes to me and says, "Remember, you are my son, Germain. You are my son. You are perfection." And my mind changes. Immediately I have a remembrance of who I am, and most importantly, what I am. And the realization and the remembrance is, I Am that I Am, divine Light, divine Strength, divine Power, divine Love, and Mother/Father God.

So, my brothers and sisters of this land, and the brothers and sisters of other lands also, that find themselves living upon this land. I would like you to know that I am also the sponsor of this land [America]. I would like you to ask yourselves another question. If I look at this land (and remember, I am the sponsor of this land, the same that my colleague Afra is the sponsor of the continent of Africa, and others are the sponsors of other continents, the beings on other continents); if I look at this land, I could say that I have been a failure again. If I looked at what is happening with the energy of war, this idea of oppression of others. I do not judge, I observe that there is an energy afoot here. If I looked at what is happening, I could say that this land is not the utopia I envisioned when I agreed to sponsor this land. But I see the perfection in the struggle. I see the wondrous opportunity given to all to move beyond the energy of struggle into the energy of Oneness.

There are politicians in this land that I communicate with continuously, and some of them are standing up and speaking of the Founding Fathers of your land, of their dream of freedom from oppression from the British government. They communicate, they show themselves the stars in the sky, in their glory and their brightness, and they remind others of the dream of freedom. Others have not yet realized the dream of freedom for this land, and they go through their due processes. The freedom that I hold in my heart and in my mind for this land is the same freedom that Mother/Father God holds for the whole of creation. I merely volunteered to help the beings of this land in any way that I could, to empower themselves in this freedom.

I ask you to understand that the struggles that manifest in any land, be it Africa, be it Europe, be it the continent of Asia, India, in all places, are a reflection of the struggles that each and every one has within them, the struggle in the heart, the struggle in the mind: "Am I Mother/Father God, am I not Mother/Father God? Can I integrate Mother/Father God, can I not integrate Mother/Father God? I am afraid, I am not afraid." All these struggles, which are the natural process of bringing each and every one to stand in their own light, we understand these struggles, for we have been through them—these ones who are known as the Ascended Masters, or commonly known as the Ascended Masters. In truth, I would like to tell you, that "the Ascended Masters" has become a generic term for a collective consciousness of beings, when in fact esoterically, not within the hierarchy, but within higher levels of consciousness, it is there that the true masters of Creation reside.

But it is true that we are ascended, and we have in the main integrated our mastery, so we do not complain about this term. We do not suggest that you do not use it. But we say it has become a generic term for a collective consciousness. But we, these beings who have taken our ascension, and have integrated our multi-dimensional mastery, we do recognize the struggles within you, we recognize the pulling to and fro of the programmings, anger from the feelings of disempowerment. It is natural, it is natural until you understand that there is no need for anger. Then anger becomes a tool that you no longer need to use. But anger can help you to stand in realizing your mastery, if you realize that it is, in the human body, somewhat natural. Note that I say somewhat natural, for it results from the feeling of powerlessness. It is understandable that when one feels powerless, that this energy rises within them. It helps ones to realize the greatness of their beings, if only they can work through it. Many struggle, and as I said, the reflection of this struggle is manifested in every land, in every race. This struggle is the struggle for perfection. The struggle for perfection.

So I, Germain, ask you to give up this struggle. I ask you not to struggle with your perfection. I ask you not to judge yourselves because you consider you're not perfect. I ask you to affirm, "I Am that I Am, Perfect. I Am that I Am, Perfect. And all my brothers and sisters are perfect in the eyes of Mother/Father God." Because you are a creation of Mother/Father God. Mother/Father God created you in his/her own image of perfection. Not perfection of body, but of perfection of energy. So I ask you to cease to struggle, cease to struggle, and BE. And love, love, love, love yourselves as if your lives depended upon it. Because in many ways, your lives do depend upon it. How many lifetimes are you prepared to spend in struggle in the future? You don't have to spend any more lifetimes in struggle.

You can spend as many lifetimes upon the planet that you wish to, showing that you realize your perfection, the mastery of life. This is one thing that I tried to demonstrate at Versailles. People wondered how I lived. I seemingly never worked. I had no income. And yet, one of my favorite things to do was to give people gifts, gifts which made them wonder about generosity and love. If I had no income, where did the gold come from? Where did the jewels come from? Where did the perfumes and other things that I gave come from? I, Germain, manifested them. I created them, in another dimensional reality, and brought them here. It is coming for you. As you manifest your dreams in other places, you can also manifest anything in other places, and bring it here into this dimensional reality.

At this time [2002], we have a number of beings upon the planet that show you that this is possible. One of them is the man we know as the Yogi Christ incarnate, Sai Baba. [Sai Baba made his transition in 2011]. Many of you, if you have never seen Sai Baba in his ashram, may have heard of the things that he demonstrates. You may say, "Why does he do this? Is it theatrical? Is it satisfying his ego? Is it because he wants people to follow him, listen to his every word?" It is none of that. He does it to show others that the manifestation of all dreams is possible here. That is why he does it. Have you noticed that sometimes he's attacked verbally, that ones create stories around him, as they have done around other masters, to try to get people not to listen to him? And yet he has nothing but a message of love and empowerment. He does not incite revolution against government. He does not incite revolution against society. He does not incite revolution against religion. He does not incite revolution against education. Why is this man considered to be dangerous, and his credibility needs to be destroyed? It is because ones are afraid of the empowerment that he gives. He gives love, pure love. Many don't understand that even when he was a boy he taught others by showing them the love inside them. His parents tried to stop him. Many of the local teachers, the Brahmins, the local Brahmin witchdoctors tried to stop him. They even went as far as trying to damage his brain. Do you know that they hammered nails into his head? They hammered nails into his head! And yet he overcame everything, and stood up and said, "Divine Love is all that's needed."

You are divine love. Be it. Bring the Goddess inside of you, and bring the God inside of you. For you are that, and this bringing in of the goddess and the god is just allowing yourself to receive the gift of your god- and goddess-ness, moving out of duality and separation. I give you instances of myself, and others who are still incarnate on the planet, like Sai Baba, to show you, "Cease the struggle! Be the dream!

Cease the struggle of duality! Cease the struggle of duality. Don't fight, because you are already."

This being, whose body I am using to speak to you through, has said to you that duality is the problem you have to find the solution to, to put it plainly. You have been told by numerous masters, numerous people willing to share, that there are no problems, only solutions. So what is the solution? I've given it to you. Be the divinity that you are. Understand that when you say, "I don't want," you don't get. And when you say, "I want, and I receive and allow," you have.

Allow the winds of change to take this ship that is your physical body home into the safety and freedom that is the Creator's love. Allow the winds of change to blow around you, and stand steadfast. Integrate the energies of the winds of change, integrate the realizations, the lessons, the gifts. But stand like the oak, solid, dependable, and grounded. The oak is so solid because it has its roots firmly in the deep of Mother/Father God. The oak says, "Throw everything at me. I am here. I radiate the branches that are me, that are beauty, whether they are covered in leaves or whether it is the winter, and I have withdrawn my energies within myself, to mediate on my solidarity, upon my connection with Mother Earth and Father Sky." Take a lesson from the oak. Ground yourselves firmly. Keep your heads open to the sky, keep your energies open to the love, the support, the greatness that you are.

I would like you at this moment, if you feel it is appropriate for you, as an individual, to close your eyes and turn within, and see the solidness of the oak that is you. Feel the roots grounding downwards into the heart of Mother Earth. Feel the roots becoming solid, spreading outwards and outwards. Feel the support of Mother Earth, holding you. For that is what happens when you put down roots. The trees stand solid because they allow the support of Mother Earth. Feel your roots going downwards, downwards, downwards, outwards, outwards, outwards.

Feel the grounding and solidarity. Feel yourselves becoming solid, integrating your energies. Solid, solid, solid. And feel your branches spreading upwards, to the stars and beyond. And feel the love and support of Mother/Father, the lifeblood of Creation flowing into you.

I Am that I Am, divinity and love in this moment, and in every moment of Creation! I Am that I Am. I know that I am loved and supported by the Universe, by Mother/Father God. I Am that I Am. I affirm I Am the power and the glory of the Divine incarnate! I Am that I Am!

KEEP IT SIMPLE—JUST ALLOW (J.A., Pathway to the Cosmic Heart workshop, 2014)

We have to go beyond the old constructs. We should, as much as we can, put aside these concepts that have been constructed, shared, or maybe you've created your own concept or whatever. As these energies that we haven't been able to bring to the planet before are now becoming manifest through you, and here to the planet, it's more constructive to not even think about grounding it or whatever. Just allow yourself to ground it.

I'd like to remind you of something we've said in the last few days about the so-called future on planet Earth. Don't create any visions or concepts of that, because then you start to construct a limitation around the manifestation of it.

We won't say "the best thing", because this creates a concept in the mind that one thing's better than another—but we have to use words to get you to understand on a 3rd dimensional level. If possible, just *allow* yourself. There's ways of triggering this allowance. We're often talking to you about affirmations, doing things through words and thoughts. You could say, "I am open to ground the fullest radiation that is possible for me to ground," or something as simple as this. You'll find that actually you become more open than you were before.

We'll share something from one of the NPMDT family. The first time I met her she came to me in a break time and said, "Hari, can you share with me any kind of technique or process or something so that I can be more aware, have a stronger contact with my I Am Presence and the multi-dimensional Presences and so on?" "Yes, I can. It's very, very simple." Now she has this smile on her face, "Now he's going to reveal the secrets of the universe to me, in break time."

"The best way to do this, love, is to notify your I Am, notify your Monad and the multi-dimensional masters, and notify the Universe, that you are open to receive."

"Oh."

On occasions, in communications with her, she mentioned this again. Just last month in an email she said, "I'd like to thank you once again, Baba, for what you said to me that time, because this works 100%. When you said that to me before, I thought, 'Oh, is this all?! But anyway, I'll do it.' Since then, my whole life and everything's changed."

This is the simplicity of it. Absolutely nothing is complicated. I know that this is part of my activity on Earth, to encourage people to keep everything simple, and not get involved in these concepts that are formed by the human mind. Because the mind can't understand all this, can't understand what's happened. When we try to understand with our minds, it brings it all back into 3rd dimension. So it's a question of moving forward in openness, and not trying to process things, pigeonholing it and filing it and relating it to something. At the moment, we don't have the reference points. We just don't have the reference points. This just hasn't happened on this planet before.

Our minds are very limited anyway. We can expand our minds in some ways, so we can sometimes understand a broader concept of things. But this part of us that we call mind isn't multi-cosmic. It can't understand even the concept of multi-cosmic. It can't understand the manifestation of multi-cosmic things. It can only understand reference points that it has in 3D, through 3D experiences.

So we're always encouraging you, don't get technical with all this. Some things are explicable in a technical manner, this is true, but once we start moving into the realms of cosmic and multi-cosmic consciousness, there's nothing to say about it from the standpoint of mind. It becomes an affair of the heart, not of the mind. And the heart doesn't work like the mind. It doesn't have the same way of processing things. It doesn't need reference points. Actually, the heart knows everything.

This is why we've often said to you in the past that there is nothing new in Creation, there's only things we haven't experienced before. Everything exists within us. Just remember, if our spark of consciousness, the Divine Self, or even this spark of Cosmic Consciousness that is behind the Divine Self or Monad, is a piece of the Cosmic aspect of the Source of this aspect of creation, well, we're everything, aren't we. There's nothing new to see. There's only a new mode of allowance into, and to move out of these self-constructed limitations.

One of the voices on the Mahatma track [CD] says the essence of it, "We'll bring freedom from the fetters of your consciousness." This is all self-constructed. Of course, there has been a great deal of assistance in this construction. So we won't lay it all on each individual. We also have the collective consciousness, as well, which is stored away in the Christ Consciousness grid. And we're all hooked to the collective consciousness. So even if we don't get completely brainwashed through the education system and our families and religion, we're still hooked to the collective consciousness. So we're being fed these constructs, in a subconscious way, and it comes into our consciousness.

This is why it's really, really important, and we're always asking you to pay attention to what you're feeding into the collective consciousness. This is why Gandhi used to say, "Be the change you want to see." As you change, it feeds into the collective consciousness. This gives every other being who is hooked into the collective consciousness the opportunity to receive the information and download it. The information isn't in concise sentences or anything like this. It's energetic imprints, which various aspects of the Self translate into knowing, or whatever, or even translate it into unknowing—but it affects us. So this is why we're always saying to you, "Please take care, please take care, and please take care."

What's happening to humanity now—I'm sure you've heard of this phrase the "Hundredth Monkey Syndrome". Let's go beyond the Hundredth Monkey label for this. This explains how things work with the interactions of collective consciousness with ourselves, and what we feed into the collective consciousness.

There's nothing really complicated about all this. It's all very simple. We could go into weeks and weeks of discussion about how this manifests into our consciousness and so on, but we don't need to know all that. All we need to know is that it does. The technicalities about it are not important. We all just need to know that it does.

What we're doing now—and it's important to understand that I'm not claiming that I'm the only one having access to what we're doing now. That would be rather egotistical. Many people are involved in these activities in different ways and presenting it from different angles, or different levels of understanding and so on. This is necessary because of the difference in the mentality of the human race. I don't know who most of these people are. I just hear bits of information come back to me, or people ask me, who've gone to these workshops, "Well, what do you think of this?" I don't know, because I didn't go there; I don't investigate this other person's work because I'm busy doing my own thing. But it's a very exciting time now, that so many other people are, as well, linking into different ways to prepare people to be open to these energies that we haven't been open to before on Earth, or they're creating energetic situations where people can directly experience it. It's a very exciting time.

I can tell you that, originally, I didn't want to do this, but that's the way my ego works. As you all know, I didn't want to do the NPMDT project either, in the late 1980's & the '90's. When this [Integration of the Cosmic Heart] was first mentioned to me two or three years ago, I was the same. "I don't want to do it. I don't want to do it. Other people are doing things like this. I don't want to do it." But anyway, here I am. This is a real illustration of how your I Am Presence and your Divine Self engineers things. "Well, we're going to do the project anyway, even if your ego doesn't want to do it. We're going to find a way of getting you."

We hope that what we've shared with you, both the Upstairs Department and what I've personally shared with you in the last half hour or so, will assist you in integrating the fact that it's necessary to allow, allow, allow, allow and not to question, question, question, question. This illustration that I just gave of our sister's, it works if you allow, you've just got to give notification. And you've not got to block it.

I could share from my own experience too, that it's not always the easiest thing in the world for your ego to stay on the case and be focused. Sometimes we get a bit sidetracked and a bit forgetful. Watch out for this forgetfulness. It seems to me, from my own experience, that it's easy to fall into this forgetfulness. It's not a question of constant neurotic self examination. That isn't going to take you anywhere either, except expanded neurosis instead of expanded consciousness. I must remember that one, it's a good one.

Ultimately we don't know where all this is going. The results are going to be distinct energetic changes on the planet, which will give us the opportunity for further understanding of the nature of our true selves—but also to break down the constructs. Like I said on the first morning, I spoke a bit about illusory reality, or about the "matrix", if that's what you want to call it. That's the trendy name, that's the disease of the period. We're stuck in the matrix!

By bringing in these expanded energies and preparing ourselves to be able to process them, this is going to break things down, break things down, break things down. Also as well, you have to expect your lives to change. This doesn't mean total destruction of your lives or whatever. But you can't live in the old way anymore. OK, you can live within your society, you can live within your relationships, you can live within the tasks that you may have chosen to interact with society, the way you make a living and so on. It doesn't mean to say that you have to destroy all that. But the way you relate to it will change.

From our hearts—of course we don't have hearts, the Upstairs Department, but you understand what we mean—we encourage you to pay attention, but don't struggle. Use this affirmation, "I'm here, I'm ready, I'm open. Bring it on!" And sure enough, it's here.

I don't know whether anybody else feels this, or if it's just for me personally, but as soon as I say, "OK, I'm open, I'm ready, bring it on!" I feel this distinct download coming into my system, into my body. I don't know if anyone else feels the change in the energy, I'm just wondering if it's general or if it's just that I've made the affirmation.

So let's do an experiment. This is all experimental, so let's do another experiment. Let's all repeat out loud, "I am ready and I am open to receive. I am ready and I am open to receive. I am ready and I am open to receive."

This is really interesting, isn't it. I'm slightly flabbergasted by it, the influx of the energy here. Sai Baba is saying to me, "Do you need any more proof of keeping it all simple?"

Quick Start Guide to Life

What's life? I once did ask.

My I Am said, "It is no task,

only if you just allow,

And don't keep saying, 'holy cow!'

Just be the one you are, in love,

ground the love from above,

be alive on earth right now,

for this moment it is what you allow."

Love all serve all,

love baba

John Armitage, 2014

WHAT SHALL WE DO ABOUT THE WORLD MANAGEMENT TEAM?—J.A.

People often ask me, "What shall we do about the World Management Team?" Love them. Forgive them. The WMT and the Controllers are actually working on our behalf. We've allowed them to do this to us, and now they're pushing us over the edge, beyond victimhood. They're actually in service to us. We have to turn it around, whether we see it from the point of view of being victims, or see the true reality of it. There's only one Creator at work in this universe, one Source. So even the Controllers have been created by Source. So they just keep pushing and pushing us, until one day enough people say, "Enough's enough! We're going to create a different reality on the planet!" This is the track we're encouraging people to go down, "Hey, let's change reality!" That's why we say the Controllers will be all right, if we just love them. Because when they no longer have anyone to control, then they can start their journey into freedom. Because they're not free. They're in slavery as much as we are, they're being manipulated by others, they're still slaves, although they think they have ultimate power upon the planet. So we have to look at it all from a broader perspective, not from our victim-consciousness point of view, that we've been programmed with.

I'm very happy with the way things are going on the planet right now, actually. It's only because we have these great communication systems. I see that now things are moving. We only have to keep up the impetus and not allow them to drive us into fear. Who'd like to join us?

There are millions of people on this planet who are assisting the grounding of the light and the love, many more beyond the NPMDT family. Many of them have a foot in each camp. But there's really cool things going on on this planet. We have a chance to create this on-going new vision of reality. It's up to us, now. Why does Source create? To experience through it's own expansion. So there's no judgment.

Understand that we create and co-create. If we understand this, then we stand in our own power and nothing can happen to us if we don't allow it to happen. If someone wants to kill you and you don't want to go, and your I Am says, "Resist!", then resist. It's OK to say, "I'm not interested in co-creating this reality with you."

CHAPTER 6

THE PATHWAY TO THE COSMIC HEART

INTRODUCTION TO THE COSMIC HEART WORKSHOP—J.A. (2014)

About two years ago I started to get some information from the Upstairs Department about this, and they were asking me to go ahead with it. Well, you know sometimes I can be rather stubborn, is the way to put it—some people call it denial—and I was thinking, "Do I really need something else to do?" But then I started to think to myself, "Yeah, actually I do need something else to do." I was starting to get in some ways a little bit bored with what I was doing, and the Upstairs Department knows they have to keep me interested. If they don't keep me interested, well then, I go off on a tangent.

Other people, as well, are doing things with heart connections. So a couple of years ago, we decided to give it a few trial runs; we just called the workshops "Multi-Dimensional Transformation."

The Upstairs Department kept pushing me and pushing me, and they said, "Right, OK, we're going to call this 'Pathway to the Cosmic Heart.' " So now I am quite excited all over again.

We'll spend some time sharing energies and activations with each other, like we've done in New Paradigm MDT workshops. We'll do a number of activations. What this really is all about, I finally found out, is actually connecting both our heart chakras. Now, for years we've been doing activities, or working with, our thymus gland, our higher heart chakra, or whatever you want to call it, and of course this has benefitted us in many, many ways, and given us an added capability to allow the love to flow. But the thing is, mostly we have been ignoring our physical heart chakras.

The realization that I have now, or the information I've been given, is that it's really important to connect these two pieces of equipment together, our higher heart chakra and physical heart chakra. By doing this, it gives us further capabilities to allow a flow of, shall we call it, expanded Divine Love.

At one time as well, we were always saying, "Open your heart, open your heart, open your heart, open your heart!" I remember saying this hundreds or thousands of times over a period of years. One thing I realized about 3 years ago is that actually our hearts are always open. Everybody's heart is open. It doesn't matter who they are. And then you can say to yourself, "Well, OK, why do people not radiate this Divine Love?" Because actually, they're blocking it. Their hearts are open, but they're actually blocking the flow. So by connecting these two heart chakras, we then manifest within us what you might call the "Cosmic Heart" or "Sacred Heart."

It's a bit like these statues of Jesus with the Sacred Heart open. I thought to myself, "Well, well, our house is full of statues of Jesus and angels and this kind of thing." We collect them. And we're always looking for things from churches that have been closed down. In these Catholic churches in France they always have statues of angels, saints, Mother Mary, Jesus, and so on. And any time we can find them, we always buy them and have them restored. So actually, we've got Jesus "coming out of our ears" you could say. Some of them are taller than me. So, the symbolism was there all the time, and we really didn't understand it. "Oh yeah, well, the Sacred Heart!" And Jesus, or Sananda, came to me and said, "Well, at last you have started to have these realizations." But you know, we all can be a bit slow, can't we.

The Upstairs Department is always saying, "Live in your heart," and, "Just allow your heart to take over the stream of your life. Don't even think about it, and you'll find that everything will change."

Well, the way we're programmed, the way that we have related to reality, or have related to the matrix, if you'd like to see it like that, because that's what so-called reality is, and the way we relate to it. We're always thinking, "What's all this about, what's all this about, what's all this about?" Also we're told, "What you think is what you get." And that you can actually create through thinking. Well, we do create through thinking. So, "What you think is what you get," this is true. I've observed this in my own life. But now what I've realized, working with the Sacred Heart, is that when we create through mind and thought, actually there's always two opposites. One side of our mind says, "OK, I'm going to create this." Or, maybe you're not even doing it on a conscious level, but you're always thinking about something, and it happens. So you can create constructive things, and things work. And then, after awhile, it seems that things don't work, things start to fall apart, in some way or another.

This is because we create through mind. Everybody knows that our brains are split in half, don't they. We've got the Right Brain and the Left Brain. So, there's always an opposite in our thoughts. There's always an opposite there, lurking in our consciousness. This is why, often we create very, very constructive things by thinking, but something happens and it all falls apart, or we start to fall backwards, and this is because the other side of the brain, the creation of the other side of the brain's kicked in.

So now I understand that we can avoid this. We can become really focused conscious creators, by creating through the Sacred Heart, or the Cosmic Heart. This is what the project is, to assist people to connect these two heart chakras together, activating the Cosmic Heart, or the Sacred Heart, and also, linking with the Cosmic Heart of Source.

So when we say "linking with the Cosmic Heart," you might say, "Well, what's he talking about now? What's this Cosmic Heart?" Most people here will understand, or have some concept in their minds, or know that there is a Source of creation, right? And some people call it Mother/Father God, God/Goddess, or the Source and so on, and have a concept of this. Of course, these concepts are not exactly real in the sense of words, because the 3rd dimensional mind doesn't have any reference points for what Source is, where Source is, and how Source actually creates through the radiation of its Love.

But another thing I've come to realize, with the assistance of the Upstairs Department, of course, is that Source also has many aspects. Most of you will know that we're living in these physical bodies in this 3rd dimensional reality, but actually we are multidimensional beings. You might not completely understand what that means, but you may have a concept that we have a presence—sometimes we say bodies—in other realities, up until we get as far as our Monadic Selves, or our Divine Selves, whatever you'd like to call it. So we've all thought about that, and we've had some kind of concepts in our minds about it, but we haven't really, in many ways, thought beyond that. We've been saying to ourselves, "If I can consciously connect to my Divine Self, or my Personal Source, the Monad, then life, or my understanding of life, God/Goddess, the universe is going to be very, very different. And I'll have a very conscious connection with Source."

So where are we going with this? I've come to understand that even Source itself has other aspects, other presences. So of course, we have to find 3rd dimensional words to explain this. We've used the phrase "Divine", we've used these other phrases to bring some kind of concept to it. Now the only phrase we have left is, "Cosmic aspects". I don't know that once we have a conscious connection with the cosmic aspects of ourselves, when we integrate the energy of the Cosmic Heart by activating the Sacred Heart and everything, I don't know what kind of phrase we're going to use to explain the next step. You know, like whether it's going to be "super-cosmic" or "multi-cosmic", "bloody cosmic" or whatever! I don't know where we're going with that. But anyway, that's for the future. At the moment, the project's to really activate the Sacred Heart and to connect our heart chakras, and to connect with the Cosmic Heart of Source. So when you think about this, it's rather exciting, isn't it. Is it?

Well, as you know, the energy on the planet keeps changing and changing and changing. Even since we were here last, or I was here last, so many things have happened, haven't they? Many people are saying that the planet's in a worse state than it was last year. I know I've said this before, but I'm going to say it again, to encourage you. Don't take any notice of this brainwashing. It's all designed to stop you from looking any further. In fact, there's less war on the planet than there has been for thousands of years. The thing is, you have it in the news all the time, because the communication systems really work very well, and the communication systems are actually used to keep the fear matrix active in humanity. It's about ramping up the fear, ramping up the fear, ramping up the fear.

I was talking to an Afghani person the day before yesterday, my taxi driver, and he said, "Have you ever been to Afghanistan?" I said, "Yeah, I have. It's a pity what happened to the country." He said, "The Americans have destroyed our country, and brought it to its knees. What for?" I said, "Well, actually there's a lot of money in war, and as well to keep the fear matrix active, always, always, always." I said to him, "My concept in all this is, we have fundamentalists in Islam, in Christianity, in Judaism, in Hinduism. There's actually billions of people living on planet earth. But the thing is, now it's all about Muslim fundamentalists, and if you live an ordinary kind of life, you're not going to run into any of these people. You're never going to come face to face with one of them. There's only a few thousand of them, and there's billions of people on the planet. And yet, they keep ramping up the fear, ramping up the fear, ramping up the fear."

So I reckon that, with this Cosmic Heart energy, we can start to dismantle this planetary fear matrix, and get people to get out of the fear of being human, get out of this fear of living in this 3rd dimensional reality. Get people with their feet on the ground, and actually, the universal ascension process will move forward very, very quickly. I mean, the universal ascension program is moving forward very quickly anyway, and when I say universal, a lot of people are actually thinking, "Well, ascension is like, for you personally, or ascension is for planet earth." Well, there is a personal ascension project for each person, and it is possible to individually ascend to your next level of ascension. But the whole project is the universal ascension. The universe is going to ascend. So by assisting in the cracking up of this fear matrix, which is really manifest on earth—and of course, the core fear matrix which is manifest inside most people—the more we can dissipate this, actually the faster, or higher frequency energy we can ground on the planet. So this really is a worthwhile project.

If you're going to ask me, "What's going to happen in the end?" I'll tell you the truth. I don't know. All I know is that the universal ascension is going forward. We've had all this talk about going to the 5th dimension. We aren't going to the 5th dimension anymore. At one time that was part of the project, but it's like all these projects in creation, it changes. First of all, they give us a concept, and we say, "OK, now we understand this concept, in a certain way, and it's always ascension to the 5th dimension." Now they say, "Well, what's the point of ascending to the 5th dimension, when you can actually ascend to the 12th or the 13th or even beyond?"

So, as we bring in more of this energy of the expanded Divinity of Love, the higher frequencies, and we ground, we have the opportunity to go beyond anything we've ever experienced before, not only in this universe, but in other aspects of creation. We're living in a gigantic experiment. We're living in a gigantic experiment. All this has never been done before. It's never been done before. I actually find it quite exciting. It goes beyond all of the previous concepts that we've had.

When I say it goes beyond all of the previous concepts that we've had, when we look at ourselves, or compare ourselves with children, you know they relate to their reality in one way, and then they start to understand how things work, and their concept of reality changes, and then they understand a little bit more, and their concept of reality changes. Well, this is what it's like for us as grownups. Ultimately, another thing that I've realized is, that—OK, I've used this phrase *the matrix*. Many of you might have seen the Matrix movies, especially the first one. The other ones weren't as good as the first one. The first one was like really to the point, and it was very understandable. But, you know, we are living in this matrix, are living in this created reality which has nothing to do with absolute reality.

So, we're living in physical bodies. What happens if we quit our physical bodies, or we go through this physical process that people call dying. Now, you hear people talking about "near-death" experiences and so on, don't you. Some of you will remember a story I've told about one of my workshop members, a woman who died in one of my workshops in Holland. I've said before, "Dying in one of my workshops, I don't allow it. I'm very easy going and patient, but I don't allow dying in my workshop." So, actually we got the woman back—well, Mother Mary did. To cut a long story short, she came back into her body and said, "I died!" And I said, "Not allowed! What happened?" She said, "I left my body, and then I saw this big tunnel of Light, and my mother and father were by this tunnel of Light, saying, 'Come on, come on!' until Mother Mary appeared and said, 'Get back! Get back in there!'" So this is how she described this near-death experience.

I remember back in the '70's, one of my girlfriends got murdered. I was very friendly with some channelers—in those days they were called "mediums" and they worked the spiritualist churches and those kind of things. It was one lady I was friendly with, she was in her late '80's. As part of my service to humanity, I used to take her shopping. I'd drive her to town to the supermarket, carry her bags, drive her home, and all this kind of thing.

So one day, we were in the car in the supermarket parking lot, and she said, "Have you lost somebody very close to you? This person was your girlfriend or something that died in quite a violent way." "Yeah, actually, it was not all that long ago. My girlfriend got murdered." She said, "I've got her here, and she wants to tell you that everything's all right, and she's now with her family, and what you described to her about death was actually the way it happened. She saw this tunnel of Light, and some of her older relations who had passed away were there waiting for her, saying, 'Come on!' It's all true."

Where am I going with all this? It's very simple. This is all part of the recycling of souls, and if you go through this tunnel of Light, with your family and all this, they're living in another illusory created reality. Sometimes people even write books about this; they channel information and they say, "Oh we're living in houses, we've got dogs and kids and this kind of thing." What? It's totally illusory. This again leads to reincarnation. So actually, going through these systems and into these illusory realities is all part of this control matrix all over again. What we need to do is to bring in some higher frequency energy, this expanded energy of Divine Love, and through radiating this through our Sacred Hearts, to dissipate this matrix that we're living in.

So you can see it's quite an exciting project. There's a part of my mind that says, "OK, I understand," and then the other part of my mind says, "Well, what's going to happen afterwards?" As I said to you, I don't really know. Somebody asked me recently, "Do you have any idea of what life will be like on planet earth once this matrix is broken down? Do you have a vision of it?" I thought for a second or two, and I said, "Well no, actually I don't." And then my I Am Presence said, "Yes, you do." So I said, "OK, yeah, I've changed my mind. I do have a vision. The only vision I have, though, is that we all live under equal circumstances, and there's no controllers. Everybody has the same opportunity. Everybody understands what human life is about, and how we should love and support each other, and see that all people are equal, and everybody has what they need." They said, "Well, how will that work in society?" So I said, "This is why I said I didn't a vision of it before, because if I have a vision of that now, actually I'm limiting the manifestation of the future." Then I thought to myself, "What did I just say?" And I sat and thought about it for a couple of seconds. And I thought, "Yeah, that's right."

Now, in the past, also, we've sat down and said, "It'll be like this," or "It'll be like that", or "It could be like this or that", but actually, again, what we've been doing is limiting: implanting these seeds in the matrix and actually limiting the way things can manifest. So what we have to do is, as I said, get away from our minds, because our minds are very limited—really, really limited. And we're always trying to relate to concepts that we have a reference point to. These reference points are in some ways not correct. I mean, they might be correct in the moment, but they're not correct in expanded reality. So let's stop thinking about it, and let's allow it. And let's not limit the creation of it, because we don't understand it. We *can't* understand it with our minds.

But the thing is, the Cosmic Heart, or the Sacred Heart, actually connected to the Cosmic Heart of Source, or the Cosmic Aspect of Source, *does* know already that our minds can't think about it. So, we're going beyond all the things we thought of. Just think about that: we're going beyond all the things we thought of. "Aw yeah, we know that—multidimensional—aw yeah, yeah, yeah." But another thing that I've realized is that, although we're multidimensional beings, and we have multidimensional presences, actually we're multi-universal beings, and we have presences in other universes. Think about that. Then you say to yourself, "Well, what are these presences in other universes, these multi-universal presences?" Again, we can't talk about it, because if we attempt to explain it in 3rd dimensional words, we're limited to 3rd dimension all over again. We can't have a concept of it. But ultimately, the Cosmic Heart knows. The Cosmic Heart knows.

So, we're asking you now to please make more of an effort, even though you've definitely been making an effort before, to allow your heart to make the decisions. Because your heart always makes the right decision, or the correct decision. Ultimately there's no such thing as right or wrong anyway. They're 3rd dimensional concepts as well. But the heart will always make the correct decision. Don't allow your mind to question the decision. Instead of saying, "Shall I do this, shall I do that, shall I do the other thing?" just say to the heart, "OK, let's take the correct path." And then it comes. Your mind—we'll just make it simple, the heart says, "OK, turn right" and the mind says, "Why?" And the heart says, "No, just turn right," and the mind says, "Yeah, well why? Maybe I should go left, instead." You know, there's two opposites again.

So, make more of an effort, or allow, allow, allow the heart to make the decisions. Ultimately, we've become so programmed in the matrix, that oftentimes we're not wanting change. The mind says, "I'm happy with the position I have in the illusion, or in the matrix." Then the emotions say, "I'm not happy, I'm not happy, I'm not happy, I want change." And the heart says, "Well, we can have changes any time." Then the change starts, and the mind says, "No, I won't, no don't. Nooooo! What's going to happen to me now? I don't want this change."

A lot of us look at ourselves as free thinkers, and we understand, to a certain extent anyway, how the control works, and so on. But then the mind says, "Oh, how will I live, what will I live on, what will happen? Yahdiyahdiya." And the heart is aching, saying, "Come ON, let's move, let's be free! Let's experience another way of living!" "Oh, yeah, but I don't want to move, I don't want to leave my town, I don't want to leave my country, my family" and all these kinds of things. "I like my job." And the heart's saying, "Don't worry, be happy. Go with the flow, and we'll take care of everything." The mind is like, "Wrrrwrrwrrrrrr."

So we're encouraging you to go beyond mind, and the limitations that we've built up through living in our heads. I understand from my personal experience that this is not always the easiest thing to do. And I consider myself, in many ways very, very adaptable, in the way that circumstances change, or my own circumstances change. If I don't follow my heart, how my I Am Presence and Divine Self takes care of things is, if I don't follow my heart, actually I wake up one day and everything's destroyed. So now, you've got no choice anymore. Well, actually you've got one choice: either start processing or move on, and see how things work. So I know this, that sometimes it can be difficult to actually step outside the comfort zone, step outside of your own personal matrix, or your own personal illusory reality that you've built up around you—and also the collective illusion. But it's step by step by step by step. The best advice that we can give you is, don't fight! As I've said, I've experienced so many different things like this myself. There've been times I've sat back and said to myself, "Why did this happen to me again?" and my Divine Self says, "Gonna listen up now? Are you going to get on with the project, or not? Come on."

INTRODUCTION TO MAHATMA & BRIAN GRATTAN
J.A. (Cosmic Heart Workshop, 2014)

Brian Grattan was the man that did all the groundwork on the Mahatma energy. It's funny though, because a lot of people don't really know who he is. He's been ascended a long time now, and he actually made it very hard work for himself. But he was very brave in all this. He only did five or six seminars on the Mahatma energy, and he wrote a book, now called *Mahatma I & II*.

Brian is, was, a very interesting person. And also as well, he was a person that created a lot of controversy, especially in his seminars. One of the things people said about Brian Grattan was that he was an alcoholic, because he often used to drink vodka during his workshops. He could put it in a water bottle and nobody would know what it was. But that was all part of the way he did things, to teach people not to be judgmental.

And he gave us this great gift, in association with Vywamus and a few of the others, this great gift of the Mahatma energy. On occasion I have channeled Brian Grattan, and just now he said to me: "Do you fancy doing a channeling?" "Brian, like what's up, mate?"

And he said, "I'd like to talk to the people about how interesting it is that things are moving on since the grounding of the Mahatma. We're going beyond it, the energy now, and Vywamus has a lot to say about this as well."

What is the Mahatma? The Mahatma energy is, you could say, the love from the Heart of Source. It wasn't until 1987 did we actually manage to create a situation on planet Earth that we could really bring this energy here and ground it.

Over the years we've had numerous attempts. When I say "over the years," of course, your 3rd dimensional mind says, "Well was it five years before, or three years before, or whatever?" But *thousands* of years before, we made numerous attempts to ground this energy, but couldn't get the vibration of the planet and the people up to a vibrational level that we could bring it here.

Remember, the vibrations had to be compatible: you know, you can't mix water and fire, is one illustration of incompatible vibrations. And so, in 1987 we made this plan; and when I say "we," it's like I'm talking about Vywamus and some of the others in the Upstairs Department, and some of us in the ground crew. We made this plan that we were going to organize a world wide event [the Harmonic Convergence]. And of course, in 1987 the internet wasn't invented, but we managed in other ways. It happened near the end of August in 1987.

The Mahatma energy is this very *pure* love without conditions. We did ground it on the Earth, with the help of this master Vywamus, and some of the others. Vywamus is not traceable in our human history or anything. He was never a human being, never incarnate like that. But Brian Grattan did a huge amount of groundwork on this, and he also gave us information on some of the Cosmic Aspects of Source, as it were, some information related to the Cosmic Day that we live within, and all this.

People say: "Well, why do you call it the Mahatma energy?" The councils suggested it. "We need something really simple, and something that can be pronounced in all these different languages that people speak on the Earth. AH! Let's call it the Mahatma energy!" I did point out to them at the time, "If you call it the Mahatma energy, we're going to create another problem, because as soon as you say 'Mahatma,' many people are going, 'Er, what's Gandhi got to do with this?'" But you know, in India we've got Mahatmas coming out of the woodwork. It's the same as Baba or Babaji— if you run across a cool guy and you like him, you call him Mahatma, or Babaji, or whatever. So we finally decided that over the years people would understand.

A few years later, Brian Grattan and Vywamus had said to me: "Please start to integrate the Mahatma energy into your activities." Like, get groups of people together. So the first time I did this, after we'd done this meditation, a guy looks in the sky and he goes, "Look! There's UFOs!" And I thought: "What?" And I look in the sky, and sure enough, there's UFOs. They came over the site—there were like six of them—and they went into a Star of David shape. Everybody was going like, "Wow, man! - Wow man, there's UFOs!" And I said, "Ah!

Ashtar, is that you?" And he said, "Yeah, I thought we'd come over and show you this is pretty cool stuff!"

So this was our first experiences with the Mahatma energy. When I agreed to take on Germain's project, they'd asked that we'd integrate these two things together, so that the awareness of the presence of the Mahatma energy is shared through New Paradigm MDT.

So that's some of the history of the Mahatma energy. It's really simple to work with. Also as well, with a lot of energies we have access to, we can actually overdo it, and we can damage ourselves, our energetic systems, or whatever. Never think to yourself, "I'm working with energy and I can't damage my energy system." This is why we always have to take care to work with our I AM Presences, Divine Selves and so on. But some people are actually resistant to certain energies, because they have a cellular memory, or some kind of memory of actually being harmed by energy, or harming others with their energetic capabilities.

But the Mahatma energy has never, ever been used to harm anybody on planet Earth, because it was only grounded in 1987. And nobody has any resistance to the Mahatma energy, nobody has any memory of anything happening to them, which they weren't happy about, we'll say; so also the energy is very, very easy to work with.

MEDITATION: OPENING TO THE COSMIC HEART
Brian Grattan through J.A.

My name is Brian Grattan, and it's not often that I have an opportunity to speak through a channel like this. In fact, it is not often that I actually would like to have an opportunity to speak through a channel like this. I do not have too many things to say to humanity, in general.

I left a legacy in my last incarnation upon your world that made it possible, of course in conjunction with others, in other realities even upon the planet, to be able to finally ground the energies of Mahatma into the 3rd dimensional reality of this world. I also as well, through my activities, investigations and my contacts with other-dimensional beings, shared some small pieces, some snippets of information, about the Cosmic Aspects of yourselves, about the manifestations of what we call "The Cosmic Day."

I wanted to take this opportunity to pass on to you a thank you, from myself and the team of beings that I still work with. Some of them you are familiar with of course, Vywamus and others, but there's many more, and there isn't an opportunity for them all to be able to gather in one voice and to pass on to people that are still incarnated in this reality, in the physical, to pass on this very, very, very big thank you. And it really is a very, very big THANK YOU.

Some people have questioned the channel and said, "Why has it taken so long, since 1987, to come to the point that humanity is at now, or taken so long to be able to interact with the energies that you are interacting with now, in these days and this gathering?" My friends, it is not long. Measured in your earth years, of course, you may relate to it as an empty period of time, but it isn't.

I encourage you to continue to integrate the fact, or even begin to integrate the notion that time does not exist in creation. It is always said there is no beginning and there is no end. There is no time frame. Some people claim that the Source, Mother/Father God, is in a hurry to complete the Ascension Process in this aspect of creation, within your Universe. Sometimes people are mistakenly saying, "We must hurry, we must hurry, we must hurry. If we don't hurry, all will be lost, all will be lost, all will be lost. We must hurry, we must hurry."

I am here to tell you that there is no hurry. For as it is constantly spoken, there is no time. So I encourage you, please do not push yourselves. Do not push yourselves, or attempt to push yourselves, way, way, way beyond the limits of what your energetic systems can handle. There isn't any need. It is also counter-productive, my friends.

I remind you that part of the core of the essence that we share with you is to be compassionate, and this does not mean living in the illusion of compassion for other beings, or living in the illusion of compassion for Mother Earth or Creation, and not living your life in compassion for the self. It has been said to you so many times, that if you think you are compassionate to others and not compassionate to yourself, it is nothing more than a self-generated illusion, through the activity of the ego.

So compassion for the self is the first thing to cultivate. As you cultivate this compassion for the self, you will understand, realize, integrate—in the very, very core of your being—that compassion for yourself is first and foremost. Now many, many beings have forgotten this. I, myself, feel qualified to speak about this subject, because I also went through the experience of this.

When I, Brian, first of all agreed to engage myself in the Mahatma project, I pushed myself and pushed myself and pushed myself. I created so many situations that were very hard to live through. I created situations which I found a lot of difficulty understanding at the time. And this also took a great toll upon my physical body, on my physical presence. I experienced imbalances, diseases, illnesses if you would like to call them that, which then, in turn actually made it more difficult for me to work upon the project and complete it.

I also as well, at one period, tortured myself mentally as well as emotionally. I questioned, questioned, questioned and asked, asked,

asked for answers to questions which I could never understand. And, as sometimes the answers never came, because there is no point in giving you answers you don't understand, I tortured myself more, because of my lack of understanding. So I do have some experience in the way that humans think, in the way that humans live, in the way that humans do things. So I encourage you to go simply and sweetly with the Mahatma energy.

It is so simple. The essence of it is this Love, and Love without conditions is composed of a number of intertwined energies. These intertwined energies you all have heard many speak of. Compassion, of course, is one. Through compassion comes non-judgment—this is two. And the Love without condition is three. Here we have again the Holy Trinity. These things, the three intertwined, will actually bring a large amount of freedom into your life. Of course, freedom—many, many speak of it, many, many seek it. And true freedom is freedom from struggling. Freedom from being afraid. Freedom from what you know as fear. This is true freedom, and when you are free, life flows in a very simple, easy, compassionate manner.

It is like an eagle or a hawk soaring in the sky. Have you ever watched them, seen them? Eagles, hawks, they live their lives, most of the time, with ease and with grace. They just allow themselves to be, and they soar to great heights without effort. Their egos don't say, "You have to struggle to get there." Their hearts just say, "I love my wings, and I will soar into the sky, completely without effort. And when I am soaring in the sky, I can stay there, still without effort, just by allowing myself to be, and utilizing the energy that Mother Earth and the sun is giving me. Of course I fly on heat, on thermals, rising from the earth, or rising from the water. I've seen the thermals spiraling into the sky, and I've become one with the thermals, the thermals take me up."

So the analogy here is extremely simple. Become one with the Mahatma. Become one, in a knowing and understanding way, with your I AM Presence, your Divine Self and your Cosmic Aspects. And actually you soar upon the energy of that, effortlessly. You ride the waves of the Cosmic Love, which will support you, again without effort. All you have to do is understand that it is there for you. And then, allow it to take you. So this is the message I bring you, a message of Compassion, a message of Love, a message of encouragement. And you have everything that is necessary to assist you.

The knowledge is there. The trigger points are spoken by the facilitators. Or they are passed on through the facilitators, by masters that have taken their various levels of ascension into multi-dimensional time and space, if you'd like to relate to it like that.

These are the trigger points. The only thing that is necessary once you see, hear, feel - or whatever the trigger point is—is to understand that the Love is there. It's constantly flowing. It is the essence of Creator. It is YOUR essence; it is nothing else. It isn't something that is mystical. There is no mystery, no secret. It is there all around. It is the flowers. It is the birds. It is the tables and chairs. It is the carpet. It is the motor car. It is everything. This is all the essence of Love. Everything that exists is based upon the building blocks of the essence of Love, which emanates from the Heart of Source.

So there's no need to look for it. All we have to do is accept it. And understand that every breath we take, every movement we make, every word we speak, and everything that happens around you, the building block or the essence of it is this LOVE. So I encourage you to understand that the Love is always around you. It is there. It is there to freely interact with. To soar upon its energies into realms of freedom that you've never dreamt were possible.

Freedom from the 3rd dimension, from the illusion of separation. Freedom from the "Wheel of Birth and Death" as it is called. Soar to new heights, heights of consciousness which you have experienced before, but you have chosen to forget. So, my brothers and sisters here, this is the brief message I bring. Remember, you don't have to struggle to be free. You already are, if you make up your mind to be.

It is very simple. It is all a question of a change of mind. A change in the way you think. Instead of "I am trapped in slavery," think, "I AM free, I AM that I AM, the Mahatma in Love."

You've been given information on the Microtron, the Microtronic Universe. This Microtron is great transmutational energy. It will transform some of the components of your physical body and your energy bodies. Electrons will become super-electrons. This will mutate the microtrons themselves, transmute, transmute, transmute everything. And when we say "transmute everything," it just means that the illusion that you may have chosen to live will just dissipate. It will go away on its own accord. You don't have to fight it, or struggle with it, because when you cease to think you are part of that, it is not part of you.

When you think that there is a struggle, when you think that it's hard or difficult, and so on, this is limiting. So my friends, soar upon the Love, soar to heights that you forget, that you have forgotten existed. Effortlessly soar on this Divine Cosmic Love. You will find that where you can go is limitless. There's nothing been said that you can only soar through this number of dimensions, or this number of feet, or this number of miles, or anything.

Remember, Source is infinite. No limitations. You are a spark of consciousness of Source. So therefore, you are unlimited yourself. So my friends, time to spread your wings, just like the eagle. The eagles can't always fly. Eagles are incarnated in eggs. The egg, the shell of the egg, is a protection for this very, very soft being. The shell, the hard shell, protects from the outside environment. And then, as the being grows within, the being says, "I am confined. There must be something else."

The shell is broken. See, now this is you breaking out of the confines, the illusion of the 3rd dimension. Then there is an emergence of the small being. And the small being is reliant on the mother and father for food—can't fly, can't find its own food. The mother and father encourage, feed, encourage. Well, this is it. You see when you break out of the illusion, you need some support, some love.

And the love and support is here. Remember, the arms of Mother/Father God are always around you. You are being held in the safety of the arms of Mother/Father God. Plus there's many other beings that have taken this journey before you. They will also come and hold you safely in their arms, and they will feed you. They will feed you. They will feed you with Love. Love, Love, Love.

"See," baby eagle says, knows, "Eat as much as you can. Eat as much as you can. Eat as much as you can. This will make you strong. Don't know what will happen to me, but this will make me strong." And the loving parents keep giving, giving, giving, giving, and the chick becomes stronger and stronger. Well, this is what it's like.

As when you say "I am open to receive—Love, Love, Love, Love, Love, Love, Love," it is brought to you. It is brought to you because you are open to receive, and you become more and more and more open, until it doesn't need to be brought to you anymore, because you're linked in with the flow. It was always there, but you didn't realize.

And then, one day, the chick says to himself, "I'm rather fed up now with being on the edge of this cliff, or up a tree. Although I'm strong, I am being well fed, I am feeling limited. There must be something else. I observe that my mother and father can soar into the sky effortlessly. I must be able to do this." So over the edge they go.

At this point, it's unknown to them what will happen next. You have to look, use their powers of observation to see that "Ah, this is it. It is these spiraling thermal energies that my Mother and Father utilize to fly high into the sky that I dreamed about."

But it is the same for you. When you get to a certain stage, forget the limitations. When you look around you, you say: "I feel confined. I feel confined upon this earth. I feel confined in my environment. I feel confined in all the things around me." Then, you may notice, through the essence of Creation, Mother/Father's love, that only from the Heart of Source, the Mahatma, that beyond this, the Cosmic Love, from the Cosmic Heart, you can say to yourself, "OK, I understand how the others before managed to reach the heights that they did, in understanding, consciousness and their inner knowing." So it's time to leave the nest. It is time to take a deep breath. It is time to say to yourself, "I am willing, I am open, and I am safe in the arms of Mother/Father God." Remember, the arms of Mother/Father God are always around you, holding you, supporting you. Mother/Father God is always whispering in your ears, "I invite you to take a Journey of Remembrance." "A Journey of Remembrance?" "Yes, a Journey of Remembrance back into the true knowledge of who you are, and what you are. For you are One with Me, and I am One with you. And we are together on a Journey."

You see, many do not understand that the Source is on a Journey, and the Source has multi-Aspects. You know, I've discovered now that the Source has a Cosmic Aspect, a Cosmic Heart. This is not the finis. There're other aspects of Source, beyond the Cosmic. You are also part of that, remember. You are a Spark of the essence of Source.

So, the adventure awaits, and we invite you to join us on this adventure. So my friends, I said that I would not take up much time. Time is nothing to me, anyway. And once I held the opportunity, I will take it and say, well I feel it's the essence to share with you, the encouragement that I extend to you. And remember, I have just invited you to join me on the next part of the adventure.

Adventure is a marvelous thing. It stimulates, it creates an energy of "I am here, now." Another thing that it is necessary to integrate is, "You are here, NOW." Not in the past, not in the future, you are here, NOW. And the adventure, living in the here and now, is very, very different than attempting to live in the limitations of the past, or the energy of the future, that you have no concept of and has not been created yet.

Living in the now in this Divinity of Love, living in the now in this Cosmic Energy, the Cosmic Heart of Source, is just another level of magic. Allow this to manifest in your hearts and minds, and you may be very surprised where it takes you—to the highest that you can soar to, to the things that you can do, that is merely a distant dream, or maybe just a desire, as a whim passing through your mind.

So, Germain has agreed with me to stand down this day. He will take his place tomorrow. He is gracious. He is gracious, he is not involved in ego, and so on. He sees that what I'm sharing with you is, if you utilize it, if you link with the encouragement, the compassion for yourselves, that this is a constructive session. So he has said to me, "Ok, Brian, I will really stand back in the queue."

So, now I am going to take this opportunity to do what in your reality you call a meditation. Going to, not lead you on a journey but encourage you to take one. This journey will be, first of all, anyway, a journey into yourself. So first of all I am asking permission from the Creator of this energetic space to be able to utilize it in this activity. And of course, it is granted without question. But again, you see, this is an illustration of, even though the answer will obviously be "yes," don't take things for granted. Be respectful to each other.

So OK, this is a journey into yourself. Now, some of you are lying down, some of you are sitting up. It doesn't matter. Please approach this in the way that you can be comfortable. First of all, I ask you to use the affirmation that you already are familiar with: "I AM that I AM, the Mahatma in Love." And to also, as well, state that you are grounding this energy through the activated chakras in your feet. ...

Now if you would like, I encourage you to ask for an infusion of the Microtron to the level of intensity which is relevant for you, but completely in harmony and balance. I bring the Microtron, a very strong grounding of it, into the vortex ...

Now invite the Microtron to interact with you on the energetic levels that are in accordance with the will of your I AM Presence, your Divine Selves, and your own Cosmic Aspects. You can invite it any way you wish; the human mind works in different ways. ...

Now I would ask you to invite the Microtronic energy into the physical heart chakra, and the thymus gland. Also invite the Microtronic energy to pass each way through the connections that connect these chakras. In other words, the energy is going to run up and down this connection. This will assist you in transmuting any residues and blockages and so on. This will, of course, pass through your Sacred Heart. ...

Now, through your intention, bring the energy of the Cosmic Heart with your Sacred Heart, making a stream of it. It may assist you to affirm, "I activate, activate, activate my Sacred Heart."

A further opened radiation of the Cosmic Divinity and the Cosmic Love flowing into the Sacred Heart, and as it radiates from the Sacred Heart, it assists you in taking the resonance of the crystalline structures in your bodies—your skulls and bones and so on, and everything that is crystalline in your bodies, which is your complete self—assists in expanding the resonance of this Love, your capabilities to accept this resonance. Love, love, love. Divine, divine, divine. I am One with the Divine, the Cosmic Heart of Source. I AM that I AM. ...

Now I'll ask you to look inwards, look within yourself and look within your Sacred Heart. Look within your Sacred Heart, the temple of your being in this reality, your temple of connection to all the other aspects of yourself in other realities, to the Cosmic levels and beyond. You could—and we'll use the words the channel uses—you could just see, feel or imagine that actually you walk through the doorway of your heart, and now you're in the temple, your own inner temple of the heart.

This inner temple can be manifest in any way which you may relate to. For remember, although all is One and One is all, you are an individual, so your temple can be anything you wish. Just ensure that it is a thing of beauty, a thing of harmony, a thing of balance, and a pleasing place to be. This is where your soul anchors. Your material scientific investigators are beginning to come to the conclusion that the soul essence anchors here, in the physical body. This is the inner temple of your being in this reality. ...

So now, within this temple, you could see or imagine that there is a nice chair or a nice seat—if you'd like, it could be a golden throne, whatever resonates with you. Now that you're in this temple, we invite you to sit in this chair, or sit on this throne, or however you would like to see it, as it resonates with you. As you sit here, actually, you're sitting on the throne of God, chair of God, throne of the Goddess, chair of the Goddess.

As you sit, just remember, prompt the memory within you, within the core of your being in this reality, that you are Mother/Father God living in this body, that there is no separation. There never was a separation. You are One—always have been and always will be.

Now invite the energy of Cosmic Love, the Cosmic Divinity from the Cosmic Heart of Source, through all aspects of yourself. All aspects of you are Divine. Anchoring in the Sacred Heart. Opening, channel which is blooming, becoming wider. At the same time, the Cosmic Love radiates from you across the world, across your earth, into all these other aspects of Mother Earth in her Divinity. Places, dimensional levels, you know of what I speak, not with mind, you know deep within. Invite the Mother to radiate this Cosmic Love, this Cosmic Divinity of Light back to you, creating a two-way flow.

Every time it flows from you, it amplifies. Your channel blooms and grows into the Heart of Mother Earth. It amplifies, it flows. In fact, the Sacred Heart, radiates, radiates, radiates across the Universe. Now let's invite all the beings in the Universe to bask in these radiations from our hearts. It's a free choice of course, it is only an invitation, just as in the 3rd dimensional reality you extend an invitation, and an individual may accept or decline.

It is the freedom granted within this Universe. Intend this radiation to flow across this Universe, to every corner of it, right out to the very edges of it. Again, send out a loving invitation to all animate and inanimate things. Bask in this Cosmic Love. If they refuse the invitations, just bless them and love them. It is the freedom of individuals. All ones are treading their sacred paths, their own journey, even though it may not seem like that to the ego. ...

So, my friends, my brothers and sisters in the Cosmic Love, I never expected to be allotted the chance to be with you in this way, and to encourage you in the form of words and energy. Now I'll stand back from the channel, stand down as we would say. As you know, we'd like to utilize the channel another day, another time, so gentleness and compassion is also necessary in these activities.

I leave you in the energy of the Divine Cosmic Love, the Divine Cosmic Light, the Cosmic aspects of Mahatma and the Microtron. I leave you to soar upon these energies. May the blessings of the Source continue to be received by you in the mode of openness. The blessings are always there. Whether you choose to accept, of course, is part of free will. So in this Love I leave you.

[You may listen to this meditation at www.johnarmitage.me]

MEDITATION WITH MERLIN
channeled by J.A. [Merlin is an aspect of Germain]

Please allow your attention to go to your Sacred Heart. [This lies between your physical heart chakra and the thymus gland, or higher heart chakra.]

Good morning, fellow magicians. This is the voice of Merlin. We are going to link with the Sacred Hearts. I'm going to take you on a journey to a place in southwest England, in the county of Cornwall. This place is known as Tintagel, and it was here that this being that you may of heard of, known as King Arthur—who was, by the way, an incarnation of Morya, or Morya was an incarnation of Arthur, to put it in the correct order—was incarnate here during a very, very dark time in planetary history, and had incarnated to do what was possible to bring in the Light, to establish the Light.

Also, as well, one of the castles that became known as Camelot was also here, as well as a Christian monastery. Now some people wonder why there are so many claims to Camelot, whether it is from the country of Wales, even the country of Belgium has places that are known as Camelot that have relations to Arthur. The thing was, Arthur was the holder of the Light. Many, many beings were not happy that the Light was being brought into the darkness of the land. So many castles were constructed, and each of these castles was known as Camelot. The reason why all were named Camelot was that if any being inquired, "Where is Arthur?" the answer was, "He is at Camelot." It wasn't possible, for some beings anyway, to know his immediate physical locality.

I, Merlin, was incarnate here at Tintagel. Arthur had been apprenticed to the monastery. Arthur thought that he was going to be trained as a monk. Maybe even at one stage in his life he would become a bishop, or even an archbishop, who would have much to say and a great influence. I, Merlin, was tasked with training Arthur in the ways of the Light, and in the ways of magic. Sometimes when you use this word "magic" people think of all kinds of ritual and these kinds of things. But it wasn't that. Magic isn't that. Magic is life! Magic is living!

Often Arthur would be absent from classes, absent from sessions of prayer and reflection. He would be with me, going through his training. Arthur was often very worried that he would be in trouble with the abbot, and sometimes wondered why he was never taken to task for his absences. There was an arrangement with the abbot that Arthur would just be under the protection of the monastery, and he was really, in all other ways, in my care and under my training.

Actually, the castles of Camelot do not exist presently in the 3rd dimension in this time and space, but the etheric Camelots still exist, as castles of vibrating cosmic Light, radiating, radiating. But one of the main places that I trained Arthur still exists in the 3rd dimension. If you ever go to that offshore island that's commonly known as England, you may go there, you may experience the energy that is still present there.

So with this short explanation, I'm going to take you on a journey. And we are going to journey there in a living energy vehicle that is collectively generated by the radiations, the energy of Cosmic Love through your Sacred Hearts. So now, please just move into a mode of allowance, a mode which puts your mind and your ego aside, and just *allow the questions to float away into multi-dimensional reality and take care of themselves. You do not need to relate to them.*

If you cannot see what I share with you, if you cannot see what I am suggesting that you may see, please do not fight, do not struggle. For all are individuals, remember, and just the mere intention of my words and your openness to receive will bring about the energetic changes that are necessary for you as an individual.

So we take the vibration of the Light Vehicle now to a frequency in which we can travel away to Tintagel in just a few moments. Tintagel is by the sea. We are going to arrive on top of the cliffs over the sea. A stream runs over the cliff here. This water is programmed with the Cosmic Divine Codes of Light. As it flows over the cliff, these codes are actually activated and released. You may be able to hear the sound of the waves breaking on the beach, the gurgle of the stream, the noise of the waterfall, and the seabirds flying overhead, because they are also moving in the energy of change. They are included in the change, the same as all beings, all kingdoms.

Smell the sea. Let us call upon the perfume of the sea into this room that we have our physical presences within. Take a deep breath through your nose. Can you smell the sea, smell the seaweed as the waves break? The scent flows in, in a more open and focused way. The energy generated by the sea, by the breaking waves, this ozone energy, also enters your nose and lifts your spirits. It aerates your blood. The circulation becomes more and more even throughout your physical bodies. The ozone turns into oxygen; your bodies begin to oxygenate. They become lighter, lighter and lighter in the physical feeling.

At the same time, these cosmic light bodies in which you have arrived on the top of the cliffs, the wind is blowing through them, the wind that is coming from the sea. The ozone has multi presences, multi-dimensional, multi-galactic, multi-universal, even multi-cosmic, just the same as everything. So this ozone, these expanded levels of the frequencies blow through your cosmic light bodies, also bringing about an ability to receive in a more open and allowing manner.

We'll stand here for awhile, and just enjoy. In your bodies, your physical bodies, continue to breathe, breathe deeply. Enjoy the smell of the sea, the influx of the ozone. Relax, relax, relax. ...

So now, my fellow magicians, I would ask you to look around to your right, and you will see there is a path leading down to the beach. This path is often very wet and very slippery. It has moss, and sometimes very slippery seaweed deposited upon it. And even in some places, when the sea is stormy, the waves sometimes wash away pieces of this path; so some places are not easily negotiable, unless you have a lot of trust and you are very sure of yourself and your footing on the pathway of life. This path represents life. In some places life is easy, in other places you have to pay attention to negotiate it so you do not fall, you do not slip.

So I, Merlin, invite you to take this pathway to the beach, and I will meet you in front of the waterfall. You could ask at this time that your Helpers and your Angels and Archangels assist you in traversing this path, just the same as you can ask them to assist you in traversing your path in life. I await your presence on the beach. ...

Welcome to the beach! Feel the sand beneath your feet. The sand is composed of crystals, silica dioxide, just like all the sand is composed of, sometimes with other elements mixed, which make different colors in the sand, maybe make pebbles and the stones present have different colors and patterns within them—part of the beauty of the manifestation of your brothers and sisters that you may know of as the mineral world, the mineral kingdom.

As we stand in front of the waterfall, the water is falling over, it is rushing down over the cliff, landing on the beach. This water contains Divine Light Codes of cosmic frequencies. Of course, you may have manifested in your light body; you may have manifested yourself wearing clothing like you do in the 3rd dimension. Remove your clothing. There is nothing to be ashamed of by your body. Remember, you are a manifestation of Mother/Father God in this reality; your body is composed of the essence of the divinity of Love, the masculine, the feminine, the Divine Mother, the Divine Father.

Stand under the waterfall. Invite these Cosmic Light Codes of Divinity to flow through the molecular structure of your light body, the composition of the energy waves, and to interact with, to activate, to become part of you. For these codes are also part of you; but they are not maybe active yet. Of course, for some they are, for some they aren't, for this is life in the 3rd dimension. It is not a reason to judge yourself or deny yourself. Remember, you are surfing the energy of an adventure into the cosmic realization that you are an aspect of the Cosmic Heart, the Cosmic Love, the Cosmic Divinity of Light.

So, now I'm going to myself stand up in the waterfall. We're going to spend a little time here just enjoying the feeling of freshness, these invigorating energies. You could also, if you wish, affirm, "I Am open to receive. I Am that I Am, the Divinity of Cosmic Love." ...

Enjoy the cosmic shower! Laugh! Sing! Kick the water around! Splash each other! Have fun! Allow your inner child to manifest in a spontaneous manner! For many, the inner child is feeling very repressed, for you are told many, many times during your growth process in the physical body into adulthood, "Don't be childish. You are growing up. Don't be childish. Life is serious. Be serious. Pay attention." The inner child is hurting within. It is saying, "I want to play, I want to play! I want to laugh! I want to be silly! I want to be a clown! I want to be spontaneous and bring joy to the world!" And your program says, "Yes, but I am growing up. I have to be serious." And then, when you are an adult, people say, "Don't be stupid. What is the matter with you? Be serious." The inner child retreats into its shell, and hurts and hurts and hurts inside you. It tends to find all kinds of ways to manifest, and have fun, and yet is repressed, often more and more and more.

I ask you, when did you last get in the water and splash each other? When did you last spend a magic moment watching the droplets of water with the sun shining through it, reflecting all the cosmic colors of the rainbow? When did you last observe a drop of water on the petal of a beautiful flower in the morning sun, and allow the wonderment and the magic that stimulates your inner child to flow into you, allow the inner child just to stare, stare, stare at the marvels that surround you in creation. So have fun, my friends. Kick, scream, laugh! Even throw each other in the pool! Splash around! Integrate, as you laugh you'll open your energies. Your hearts will scream, "Expand in allowance! Expand in allowance! Expand in allowance! I am open to the magic of life!" So we will leave you to play for a short time, and then we will invite you to the next piece of the cosmic adventure. ...

So, now again, look to the right. You will see the entrance to a cave that is, even in this day and age, in the 21st century, still known as Merlin's Cave. It was in this cave that I passed on a lot of instruction to Arthur and also facilitated a lot of activations of his energies, expansion of his awareness.

So let us go to the cave now. As you walk in, you will see that the rock is black, and running through this black rock are white lines, and in some places, big manifestations of whiteness. If you look on the floor beneath your feet, you will see it is covered with pebbles of black with white in them. The white is the quartz. The white is resonating with this Divine Cosmic Love from the Cosmic Heart.

I invite you to stand in a circle with your backs against the wall. Pay attention to your feet here, the feet of your light body shall we say. Of course, this is a metaphor. We encourage you to just pay attention to your grounding. In a moment I, Merlin, will activate the quartz. It is already pre-programmed for cosmic consciousness and all that is necessary to assist beings in the realization of their cosmic selves, to assist beings to bring to this reality the energy of the Cosmic Heart, the Cosmic Love, the divinity of the Cosmic Light.

So, I now activate the quartz. Activate, activate, activate! I wave my wand, and the result is instant. ... Do you feel it? Do you perceive it? Allow your perception. Don't question, "What should I feel?" Affirm, "I am open to feel," and you will. If you keep asking, "What should I feel?" "You should feel nothing," is the answer. It is not a question of "should," it is a question of allowance.

So please, allowing, allowing, allowing, and I will activate the quartz to the next level of radiation of this divine Love, this cosmic Love from the Sacred Heart. Divine cosmic Light, the Cosmic Divine Light, the Sacred Heart. Activate, activate, activate! ... I invite you to put yourself in openness in a mode of, "I am open to receive, I am open to receive, I am open to receive." ...

Now I open the energy vortex, connect it with the galactic center, moving onwards and upwards in vibration, and going beyond the Heart of Source, linking with the Cosmic Heart of Source. And the energy vortex that comes through the roof of the cave starts to bring this energy of Cosmic Love, Cosmic Divine Light into the energy vortex. And the energy vortex spins off these energies, and reflects into your Sacred Heart, if you would choose to allow that. And the connections between your physical heart and the higher heart chakra become more enhanced, more enhanced and more enhanced. And the two-way flow between these two chakras further brings an activation to your Sacred Heart. And your Sacred Hearts reflect to each other within this vortex, and then the vortex very simply spins off this energy, and as it spins off, spreads it across the earth. It makes this energy of the Cosmic Heart and the Cosmic Love available to all beings of all kingdoms, to those who are open to receive.

So I keep on bringing the energy of the Sacred Heart, the Cosmic Love, this divinity flows, flows, flows. And now, from the vortex there appears a chalice, a cup. It is the Holy Grail. Many are searching for the Holy Grail. Many have searched the earth for the Holy Grail. There are legends that the Holy Grail exists in numerous places. I will tell you, my friends, that the Holy Grail is within you. Each individual has the Holy Grail within. This is the chalice inside you, the chalice that holds the Divinity, the Love.

You could say that the base of the chalice is anchored in your solar plexus, and the cup of the chalice is at the position of your physical heart chakra. Your higher heart chakra and the Sacred Heart dwells within the chalice of Love. This manifestation of the perfection of Mother/Father, this chalice that rises from the vortex—you can choose how it manifests to you. It can be plain, made from wood. It can be made of clay. It can be made of gold, silver and other precious metals and encrusted with jewels of all kinds. You choose. ...

And the Cosmic Love of the Cosmic Heart, from the Cosmic Heart of Source flows into this chalice. It fills the chalice, and the chalice overflows. You see, there is an overflowing of the Cosmic Love, an overflowing of the Cosmic Divinity, the Cosmic Light. There is no limit to it.

It is always overflowing, overflowing in your lives, in your 3rd dimensional lives, overflowing into the heart of Mother Earth. Sometimes we choose not to perceive this flow and this overflow. Sometimes our eyes are closed, our inner sight is also closed, just because we have allowed ourselves to manifest the illusion in our minds that we are separate, that we are separate from Mother/Father God, from the Divine Feminine, the Divine Masculine.

As the chalice overflows, the energy goes into the vortex. And as it spins off out of the vortex, it flows into you as well, into infinity, and the Holy Grail within you fills to overflowing also. And the Cosmic Love from the Sacred Heart flows through all your body, your light body, your etheric body, your emotional body, your physical body. And then it overflows into your multi-dimensional presences, your multi-dimensional bodies. And the flow becomes more fluid. As you allow yourself to receive, the flow becomes easily more fluid.

We will spend a little time here. Again, you could affirm your openness, if you think it may assist you: "I affirm I am open to receive the Cosmic Love from the Cosmic Heart of Source. This Cosmic Divine Light is permeating the whole of my being. I Am that I Am." ... ...

OK now, we are going to leave the cave, and we are going to go up to Camelot. So let us thank the keepers of the cave, and let us take with us this essence of our true selves, the Cosmic Light, the Cosmic Love. Immediately we move upwards through the roof of the cave, and we come to the castle of Camelot, this multidimensional construction of Light, Divine Light, that has always held a cosmic vibration. For many times we have chosen to ignore it. We have not seen it because our inner eye is not attuned to the cosmic vibration.

Let us walk through the doors into the Great Hall. The Great Hall is constructed according to sacred geometrics. These cosmic sacred geometric configurations are pulsating, vibrating to this cosmic Love of Source, cosmic Divine Light. You are invited to see, visualize, imagine or pretend if you like, that in the middle of the Great Hall is a very large round table. This is the cosmic vibration of the table that the knights of divine Light sat around, when they were bringing in the vibrations of Light and making plans to expand the vibrations of this table, this table constructed of cosmic crystal.

This table is inviting you to take a chair and sit around it, all of you. Originally there was only space for twelve, but now it can expand at will, so there is no limitation as to how many can sit around it. The table itself is quite high off the floor. The table adjusts itself, so the top of the table is just level with your Sacred Heart. The Cosmic Love, the Cosmic Light flows out of the table into your Cosmic Heart. If you are open to receive, it flows and flows and flows. Your inner child affirms, "Yes, yes, yes! I am further open to receive!" and starts to smile with a happy smile. The eyes of your inner child start to open wide, wide, wide in wonderment and sparkle with excitement. I invite you to sit for a while. … …

Now, at one time in this place I would have invited you to stand in front of the crystal stone that holds the crystalline sword that is known as Excalibur, and invited you to extract the sword, and for you to be gifted with a sword of Light, for each individual. But now I am not going to extend this invitation to you. If you wish, of course, you may stand in front and receive the energy, for also Excalibur does radiate this energy, and you could invite this energy into your energetic systems, into your hearts. But it is no longer necessary to possess a sword of Light to cut away the darkness, because as you allow your Sacred Hearts to shine, the darkness does not need to be cut away, it just transforms into harmony and balance.

Light and dark are necessary. If there was no darkness, you would not know Light, and if there was no Light, you would know no dark. It *is only in the shadows that the imbalances exist. So with the emanations from your Sacred Heart, the Light and dark comes into balance and harmony, and the shadows are eliminated. It's no longer necessary to use a sword to cut away these shadows.*

We are now going to leave the Great Hall. We are going to take a little journey further, step outside. As we come outside on the top of the hill, I have invited some of our cosmic friends to be with us. You have maybe heard, in the tales and the myths of humanity, that there was a time that dragons were our friends, or some dragons were our friends. These dragons could fly, and they had the energy to bring about transformation in all kinds of ways, even by breathing fire.

Some of you may have been dragon riders. You worked on behalf of the Cosmic Love, the Cosmic Light. You soared into the sky on the backs of these dragons. Some of these myths and memories of your human race have been reflected in these things that they produce called movies. They are being recreated to inspire you to remember that blanket judgment of the reptilian beings is not a balanced way, for many interact with you with love in their hearts. Many are loving, and these dragons are a part of them.

We invite you to choose your dragon, for you know one and one knows you. You are familiar. Climb upon the back of your dragon. I will not ride a dragon this day, for I know how to fly through the universe without dragons. I will do this just to demonstrate to you that this is possible. Remember, I, Merlin, was also a human being, who also can fly unfettered through creation. I will lead the dragons, although they know where we are destined to head now.

We'll soar into the sky. As we soar into the sky, I invite you to look downwards. Down below us you will see silver and gold energy lines snaking across the landscape, from here at Camelot to this place commonly known as St. Michael's Mount. This St. Michael's Mount is a very sacred place. The energy of Michael the Archangel is present here. He projects his energy through the vortexes here to assist humanity.

He has invited us to, not to land on this little island, but to congregate in the sky and allow the radiations of our Sacred Hearts to just flow down into the lines that snake around this sacred island, these lines that hold the energies of the Divine Mother and of the archangel known as Michael. We are invited to allow these emanations from our Sacred Hearts to flow into this amplifying vortex, and it further flows into the Michael-Mary line, or the dragon line, as it snakes across the land. We follow it, and as we follow it, we see it lighting up, brighter and brighter and brighter in front of us, faster than we can move. This is the energy that we have grounded at St. Michael's.

Very quickly it appears in Glastonbury, and the Sacred Tor. On top of the Sacred Tor is a tower known as St. Michael's Tower. It exists in the physical also. You may visit it. This tower is the center of the energetic vortex of the Tor. We're going to land our dragons on the Tor. They love being here, in the energy of the dragon line, the Michael and the Mary. We're going to go inside the tower, although in the 3rd dimension maybe no more than twelve of us could sit in there, but in our cosmic light bodies we can fit as many as necessary, for we will just expand the girth of the tower.

So let us congregate there, sit. Let us activate our Earth Stars, and the chakras beneath our feet, also. Bring this open and widest radiation possible of this Cosmic Love from the Cosmic Heart into the dragon lines here. From here, many energy lines radiate out across the land, connecting with other sacred places like Stonehenge, Avebury, the Goddess Sanctuary on the ridgeway, Silbury Hill, and other places further up the country. It continues to flow up the Michael-Mary, and in the end it comes to where the Michael-Mary meets the sea, near the city of Norwich.

We continue to ground, ground, ground, allow, allow allow. The energy flashes across the sea. It arrives at a place called Mont San Michel in France. This again is a St. Michael's Mount. This divine Love, this Cosmic Love, Divine Light flows in there, into the energy vortex, and flows out across the land of France, across Europe into Russia, and then again out into the sea. It continues across the earth, activating the sacred places, so many places I do not have the energy to name them. The energy of the Sacred Heart manifests.

So here, my friends, I, Merlin, am going to say my good-byes to you. There is only a few short sentences that remains to share. It is again a reminder that you are the magicians, you are the alchemists of change. In the old days, the alchemists were looking to turn base metals into gold. They were sidetracked. They didn't know that the project was to change base consciousness into the knowingness of the Cosmic Divinity and Love. So you are also alchemists. You are engaged in alchemical processes, changing the nature of your reality, or the components of your bodies in so many different realities and dimensions. This is alchemical.

May I remind you also to remember to allow your inner child to play. Remember to sing, dance and be foolish. Remember not to judge yourself. As many have said before me, remember to sing like there is nobody around. Remember to dance like nobody is looking. Free yourself of the limitations that you have built up around you, in what you are supposed to be, and the way you are supposed to act, as a spiritual being. Spiritual beings are free; they are not restricted by some kind of 3rd dimensional ideas and concepts of behavior. So allow your spirits to be free. Surf the waves of cosmic Love. And most of all, enjoy, enjoy, enjoy.

NEW PARADIGM MULTI-DIMENSIONAL TRANSFORMATION

Thank you. Thank you for putting aside time to listen. Thank you for taking this journey with me, to these beautiful places. There are many beautiful places upon planet earth. Nature is a magical thing. But remember, you are also a thing of beauty. You also are a thing of beauty, an individual manifestation of the Divine Cosmic Love of Source. So remember, please, to look inside your heart and the temple of cosmic light that exists there. I love you.

OK, so now we're going to activate our Cosmic Light Vehicle and come back to the place we left from, integrate ourselves with our physical bodies, and don't forget, be gentle. No hurry. No hurry.

[You may listen to this meditation at www.johnarmitage.me]

Out of Illusion Into Love

Cosmic love here and above,
I see in my mind the image of a dove
bringing peace on earth with all its might
to lead us out of this dark night,
from strife and war, and loads more.
Peace on earth is at your door,
it's knocking loud and landing a few kicks,
even throwing some big bricks.
Have you seen it in your own life,
once you cut the illusion with a knife,
the sword of Michael is here for you,
to cut out all that is askew.
Remember, you are not the story,
you are of the Source in all His/Her glory,
so you are love and no more,
you can't just shut this in a drawer,
try as you may this is sure.
It is the way we are lead
out from the land of walking dead
into the land of I love life.
From now on there is no strife,
just a life of love and all that is.
Really it's too good to miss,
inner bliss.
So just laugh and smile, for you are love.
Please do not forget the dove,
for inner peace brings peace to all,
allows us all to walk tall.
So just be love, because you are.
love baba
John Armitage, 2014

CHAPTER 7

FOUNDING THE SCHOOL
OF ESOTERIC SCIENCES

In the beginning of this system of teaching, in the mid 1990's, Germain would say that all this was "copyrighted by the Ascended Masters" and Baba would tell us to "be sure you copy right!" Unfortunately, quite a few people did NOT copy "right", that is, with integrity and understanding. Some got into their egos and ran with them, changing or re-creating the message and teachings that Germain meant to pass on to us. One decided that her attunements were of a higher caliber than those of other teachers. Another person decided that she was the new head of the project, that Germain had "chosen" her to take over from John. She offered attunements on line for around $500. Germain has said that he has nothing to do with her teachings. A few others were offering activations on E-Bay in England, 15 minutes for 15 pounds.

Other problems that came up involved people just giving attunements, rather than doing the clearing meditations first. The clearing meditations are a very important part of these teachings. You can't fill a clogged up space with Light. Germain also wants the classes to involve a certain length of classroom time, because he says, "It takes some time for us to help people move beyond their denial, their resistance".

These teachings started off in the mid 1990's as a series of initiations or activations given in 4 levels. We soon moved beyond that way of doing things. This is a dynamic system, constantly growing and changing, as we, too, are constantly growing and changing. Sometimes humans have trouble with change, even fear it. Anything that does not grow stagnates. Any system of knowledge that is not constantly expanding is not worth doing.

Germain looked at what was happening with Shamballa and saw what was working, what wasn't, and what needed adjustment. He wanted also to protect the teachings from misuse and false representation. Finally Baba agreed with Germain that the teachings needed some protection in 3D in order to maintain their integrity. No one is happy that this has proved to be the case, but it has. As Germain has told us, water without boundaries will flow away and dissipate; whereas banks or boundaries will create a pond that can be useful and not fade away.

In 2004-6 Master Germain and Baba created a new way of teaching, of passing on the teachings of freedom and love, with some firmer guidelines. These are all to increase the chance of people actually learning about their freedom, their God/Goddess-ness, their innate condition of Love without conditions and Joy. Germain wants his teachers to teach the material as he has presented it to us, to bring through the energies that he has brought in for us, NOT SOMETHING ELSE. If people are going to teach something else, then they will not do it in Germain's or Baba's name, and they must call it something else.

When we had to change our name, to avoid a prolonged and expensive copyright lawsuit, Germain and Baba saw that this was also an opportunity to move beyond all the fakirs, the ones who gave lip service to the teachings but were not part of them, were not coming from the heart, in conjunction with the true objectives of whole system.

Germain and Baba created the School of Esoteric Sciences, with specific courses, certifications, and teacher trainings. New Paradigm Multi-Dimensional Transformation, as taught according to these guidelines, is now recognized by the BCMA (British Complimentary Medicine Association). There is more about these courses and how to find legitimate teachers in the chapter "NPMDT Courses, Teachers, and Contacts", as well as on our website, www.new-paradigm-mdt. org .

ON CHANGES TO NEW PARADIGM MDT & CHANGE IN GENERAL—J.A. and Master Germain

Here are the reasons behind the changes in the structure of NPMDT classes. Please read carefully, and I will use plain English so there is no mistake or misunderstanding. The list I am going to give is not in order of importance; *it is all important.*

FIRST, content of course: this is put together to make it easy for people to understand how life works and the way we disempower ourselves through non-LOVE and judgment. NPMDT, using the energies of Shamballa, is a way of life, living in Love, in freedom from fear. Oh dear, we used the F word again, LOL.

SECOND, trained and approved teachers: this helps to make sure that the people who do the courses get what they paid for, i.e. Basic Master and so on, not some off-the-wall version that leaves out the important stuff mentioned above. Some won't even do clearances for some reason, or are afraid to talk about certain subjects. Come on, let's get real and not taint things with our own fears.

THIRD, the content given by properly trained teachers gives NPMDT a professional face to the controllers, insurance companies and the rest of the 3D stuff we need to comply with in some places.

FOURTH, the activations given in an easy way take us away from the old Reiki idea. The people get activated by their own I Am; the teachers just create the situation for this to happen. NPMDT is about assisting people to stand in their own power, remember (see point one).

FIFTH, both myself and Germain are fed up with the widespread abuse of this system, by some who are determined to steal it and use it for their own ends, whatever that may be. People use my name and Germain's to trick folk into believing they have had NPMDT, when they have not got it, and so on. My channelings are used to back up their story; many say that what they give is channeled by me, but it is not what Germain gave us.

SIXTH, the last point is, all this we have put into place is to get everybody who is teaching on the same page of the book, so to speak; to be professional and be true to the energy and information Germain has asked to be given to people. No symbols that can harm folk, no outdated energies, people getting activation from their I Am and not the ego of the teachers by judging what folk need, no levels in it so people can hold onto the energy of others for personal power and gain.

Our last words are, if you don't like the way we are asking you to do things, don't complain, go and do something else. If you don't like the information given, leave it, why fight it? Have you not integrated the essence of it all yet? Just move on. If you think my channeling is shit, don't complain to me, just leave it, do something different, move on. I have no problem with that. DON'T CALL IT NEW PARADIGM MDT THOUGH. I just love you.

We are a force of LOVE, if we choose to be, and through our love, each and every one of us, we change things from within. This manifests outside of us, and the controllers come into love as well; they are in slavery as well, remember. Let's get this planet into the Confederation of Free Worlds, get out of this slavery to governments, money and ego, manifest the true us. As a reminder, we are all God and Goddess and therefore perfect now. Just wake up and dream, shake off the blindfolds from our eyes and minds, and see what life is really about on this planet. Again we ask, anybody prepared to join us? And again, if you are not, that's fine as well, just don't try to stop us; it is impossible. Nothing and nobody will stop me from fulfilling my mission, and Germain says the same thing.

OK folks, here it is from Baba's I AM Presence and Germain. Germain is the sponsor of the system of empowerment and freedom known as New Paradigm Multi-Dimensional Transformation, and I, Baba, am the person who grounded this system into 3D. Germain says:

First I would like to say there is no OTHER system of freeing people from fear that has been sponsored by me, Germain, that is known as NPMDT. Why would I do that, if the energy of Shamballa is freedom? There is nothing else in creation other than freedom worth spending time on. Yes, freedom in LOVE. Of course, I am not saying here that there is no other way to achieve freedom, for that would not be true, and it would be control. There are many ways to achieve freedom, it's true; but again I tell you none have been or are known as New Paradigm Multi-Dimensional Transformation (NPMDT)!

Shamballa energy is the energy of freedom, the essence of Mother/ Father God. How can I add anything else to that? It's impossible. As a result of this freedom, people can also help others into freedom as well as themselves, and as part of this freedom, also heal themselves and facilitate healing for others as well. Remember, wholeness is LOVE without conditions, and living in this LOVE frees people from fear. Easy eh?

I, Germain, am not Lord Germain or St. Germain, I am Germain. I never was a saint; this word was part of my name when I was living in France. I am not a saint now, either. I don't think the Pope would approve of my activities of freeing people from fear, really; no fear, no control, and if you ain't afraid of the devil, religion can't control you.

Let me tell you a bit about channeling. First, about we beings who are known as the Ascended Masters. That term is really incorrect, but we will use it here, for many have come to know us as that. But do not think we are Lords or Masters of anything, except ourselves. Yes, we have achieved a level of Mastery over ourselves, and nothing more. We do not rule the earth from some other dimension or place in time and space. We do not call ourselves Lord anything or Saint anything, for we are, many of us, just like YOU, working on our path to total freedom, our cosmic ascension and onwards, to realize our Godselves.

So we don't contact channelers and tell them we are lords or masters. We give our names. We don't expect humans to use those terms in reference to us, either. "Why do people do it?" we ask ourselves. The conclusion we have come to is that many humans are desperate to give their power away to something outside of themselves, and because we are easy to contact, they try to give it to us. We inform you all now, on planet earth, that we don't want or need it. Take your own power into your own hands and heart. You are all God and Goddess now and always were. Another thing is, you always will be. You are all going on to your cosmic ascension. It may take another few million years, but you are; you will move on to be creators of universes and worlds as well as beings, and so on.

So stop searching. Look within and be free.

We do not make decisions about the future of the earth or her children. Here, I mean all beings incarnate, humans, animals and everything. YOU make the decisions, the people of earth. YES, YOU make them. Stay in fear and denial and project your fear, and what do you manifest on earth? WAR and STRIFE. Yes, it is the projections of the human mind that cause the trouble, not some so-called dark beings from some other place. Yes, sometimes others are involved in the strife, that's true. Their place is to help you to see your creations and help you to create the outward manifestation of them.

"Why," you may ask yourself? To push you into standing in your own power, of course, and when all are in their power, they move on into freedom as well. It is the natural way of all beings in creation.

WE [the multi-dimensional masters] don't do channelings that create fear, we don't look down on others, and we don't stroke people egos and make them feel important. We just LOVE, and suggest to you folk in 3D ways you may free yourselves with the least amount of trauma and processing.

So, New Paradigm MDT is the energies of Shamballa, no frills, no symbols, no fear, and no control. Just freedom. There you have it.

LOVE to you all, the Violet Tribe, the children of the new [true] Israel, the NPMDT multi-dimensional tribe; be free, look within for your truth and follow your heart.

In LOVE, service and anything you may want, Germain, sponsor of New Paradigm Multi-Dimensional Transformation.

LOVE, Baba, founder of the above in 3D.

LOVE is the answer to fear. Don't give your power away to anybody or anything. You are everything in creation NOW. Just wake up and dream.

CHAPTER 8

THE ENERGY OF SHAMBALLA CHANGES LIVES
Stories from the NPMDT Family

MY INTRODUCTION TO THE ENERGY OF SHAMBALLA

Phyllis Brooks (Wendell, MA, USA)

It was spring of 1998, and I had just gotten connected to the Internet. I was searching for spiritually oriented websites, when I came across some channelings from the Ascended Masters, through Carolyn Fitzgerald. I started reading them and felt that they were right on. Some channelings twist your gut when you read them; others make you feel encased in Divine Love. These were the latter kind. [I later found out that she was a friend of John Armitage and had been taught to channel by him].

During my reading, I kept coming on words in blue. I soon found out that by clicking on these I would suddenly find myself elsewhere in this mysterious Net, where the word would be further explained. I did this with *merkaba*, and ended up at an advertisement for a workshop in the Boston area, facilitated by a guy called G.S., and another called Haridas Melchizedek. I had never before been drawn to workshops on merkaba activations, but the name Haridas Melchizedek called to me, so I talked a couple of friends into going to the workshop (I had to borrow some of the money from one), and we set off.

During a guided meditation at this workshop, when I had my eyes closed, the man named Haridas suddenly appeared before me in my vision. He just looked at me. Later I was talking with him when I realized that this was the person I wanted to study with. I had been looking for someone to learn from, but none of the people advertised in all the spiritually oriented magazines and newsletters of the day caught my interest. I guess I should say caught my I Am's interest, for I was soon to learn that I had a Higher Self that had never forgotten its identity within Creator/Source, and this was called the I Am Presence.

They mentioned that the two of them would be teaching a 9-day intensive in Mt. Shasta, CA in the fall. Immediately a bell went off in my head, "I'm going to go to that". I had no extra money at the time; in fact I still owed my friend for lending me the money to get to this workshop. But I KNEW that I was going, and a few days later I got an opportunity to send some of my crafts to a wholesale show. The resulting orders made it possible for me to register for the Mt. Shasta workshop. Later I found out that is how true manifestation works: you KNOW without a doubt that this is what is, and so it is. Once you KNOW, you've already created it.

During my wanderings on the Internet, I had also found a chat room where a woman was asking about "spiritual DNA". I wrote to her and we found we had a lot in common. We began corresponding. A few months later, when I told her I was going to Mt. Shasta for a workshop, she said, "I live in Mt. Shasta! Why don't you stay with me?!" So I got to meet her, and as I was attuned to Shamballa energies in the workshop, I would go back to her place and teach her and attune her as well. It was a great way to learn! The next year she took the same workshop.

This is the way my life has been going ever since. When I pay attention, synchronicities happen. The Mt. Shasta experience was life-changing. I had no plans to teach when I set off for Mt. Shasta. I was going because I was "told" to go by my I Am. In Germain's parting talk to us through John, he told us that we should not expect to be able to go home and just take up our lives where we had left off. We had changed. On the plane ride home, as I looked out the window at the multitude of tiny lights in the cities below, representing millions of people, I felt a rush of love fill my heart. I just wanted to share the joy that I was feeling. I wanted to share the energy of Shamballa with everyone who wanted it.

Don't get me wrong. The workshop was not all light and roses, although there was a lot of that. Old stuff I didn't even know about came up for clearing, and this happened almost constantly. Some of it was extremely painful. But there was always the unimaginably beautiful and bright Light that came to fill the spaces, as I released the old pain and suffering—many lifetime's worth I am sure.

I later found out why I had not been particularly interested in merkaba activation workshops before this, and that part of the teachings, and G.S., fell by the wayside for me. The path of Mastery is laced with lessons in discernment. On the other hand, the Shamballa energies opened me up to my true Self. I felt my own power, beyond any doubt or denial. I felt I was on the way to Mastery, the only true kind, which is mastery of one's Self. I wanted to spread the freedom, the light, the knowledge of who we really are. I wanted to help others step out of fear into love.

Since then, I have been teaching this modality in all of it's many transformations. For the energy of Shamballa, now the New Paradigm MDT, is an energy that grows with us. As humanity becomes ready for more light, more love, more transformations, it is there to give it to us. I had been a Reiki master when I set off for Mt. Shasta. Although I greatly respect Reiki and its practitioners, there is no comparison I can make between those energies and the energies of Shamballa. Of course, we also learned that Master Germain, who is responsible for bringing us these energies through John Armitage, was also the one responsible for the original Atlantean system of 22 symbols. It was from a few of these symbols, preserved in Sanskrit writings, that Dr. Usui created the Reiki system of the last century. So it's all in the lineage, growing with humanity and the times. NPMDT expands the freedom and the love. It's been quite a journey, and continues on, in love and light.

CALL TO COSMIC ALIGNMENT IN ICELAND

Lilja Petra Asgeirsdottir (Mosfellsbœr, Iceland)

[Excerpts from an account of J.A.'s workshop in Iceland. See Lilja and Elli's website for more tales of their adventures: http://www.geocities. com/lillyrokk]

While we were in Reykjavik, Das took a look at the mandala in the city centre and took the vortex up to the twelfth level.

We headed to the volcanic crater of Grabrok. Earlier this year Mark, Phyllis, Elli and I had worked to activate the fire there. Now it was time to activate the fire inside everyone in the group. We were all alone up on the crater and could enjoy the view and the silence before settling down in the centre of the crater to meditate. Not a very comfortable sofa, as one or two in the group thought they needed better grounding when they slid down on their bottom part! We didn't feel the cold while sitting there and working with this fire, blending it with the silver violet flame of Germain.

After awhile we went to the waterfall Glanni. At first, we just sat on some stones in the river just below the waterfall, to feel the energies and the cleansing effects. Then we went up above the waterfall where we could sit on the grass while Das channeled the Goddess energy of this place.

The glacier Snaefellsjokull has for a long time been thought to be one of the main energy points on Mother Earth, with connections to Giza. It is also the home of the mountain deva, or mountain king as we sometimes call him, a magnificent being of light. We had learned that it would not be possible for us to go to the top of the glacier, after all the rain and warm weather of the past few weeks. So we drove up to the mountain as far as possible into the snow. There we stopped the car and found a place on an energy line to work on. The channelings and activation that took place there really knocked the socks off Das.

The day after, it was time to go to Snaefellsnes again, and this time we were going on a boat trip. In the morning, I got guidance to take another route than before, and when thinking it through and talking to Das, I knew it was so that we could do some earthwork on the way. I have found out that if I dislike or don't like very much certain areas of our country, it often turns out to be occupied by brothers and sisters [on other dimensional levels] that have chosen another path in their life then we have. So this time Das got to sit in front and I was behind, while Elli was the secure driver all the time.

And sure enough, when we were driving over the mountain, we started feeling the heavy energies. Just after I mentioned it to Das, he decided it was time to stop and get out of the car. There was a base of some extraterrestrials in the mountain ahead. After we started the work, standing in a circle with Das in the middle, the beings saw that there was no way around this. Their time there was up, and they gave up without any struggle.

In another mountain close by, there was a huge extra- terrestrial crystal that Das reprogrammed. When it was activated with the love energy, all the [space] ships that were hanging around went like fireworks away and disappeared

In the afternoon we went to a cave. A few in the group had dreaded this day ever since they had registered for the workshop. We were going to have to crawl through a tunnel on ice. The cave, Vidgelmir, which we were going to, is the second largest lava cave in the world: almost 1600 meters long, with ice formation and stone formations. To get there, we needed a guide, since it is locked so that it will not be damaged. Well geared with helmets and lights, we were ready to go into the earth. Everyone in the group decided to at least start this trip into Mother Earth, Gaia.

We had to go down a rather steep path full of loose rocks. Our guide then secured a ladder into the ice, so that we might get down to where the tunnel was. He went through first, to open the gate, and the rest of us came crawling on our hands and knees after him. On the way, some stopped in fear, but were coached through it all the way. With wet hands and knees we came through and were able again to stand up. A large cave opened up in front of us. There the floor was icy, so it was as if we were out on skates. The only light came from the small lights we had in our hands, and from the bigger light that our guide had. He told us how this cave was formed in a volcanic eruption, when the lava had run through there and left this gap in the lava.

After some 50 meters, we came to a blockage in the path. It was full of rocks. We had to climb over them to get to see more ice formations, and we really wanted that. When we had managed to crawl up and down again over the icy rocks, we found a place to sit and do a meditation. This time it was time to do the cosmic alignment. This was a new cosmic energy without any disturbing energies that are on the surface of the earth. For those that could see the lights, it was a marvelous lightshow; the energies were once again very high.

THE BEE STING

Al Valcourt (Hampden, ME, USA)

One never knows how our higher selves are working in conjunction with the universal worlds, guiding us and sometimes pushing us to take steps along our individual pathways. My wife, Linda, and I met and married in the late seventies. Then we raised three sons, built our own home and worked at our full time jobs for around twenty-five years. Along the way, Linda would make crafts and pieces of jewelry. It wasn't long before we were selling our surplus pieces at a few craft shows. It's from one of these shows and our enjoyment of meeting people that eventually opened us to Reiki and then NPMDT. It is from this point that my NPMDT stories and lessons begin and blockages begin to clear.

The Machias Blueberry Festival in Machias, Maine offers hundreds of crafters and vendors the opportunity to display and sell their wares, while making new friendships along the way. It was at the end of the second day of the show and time to pack things away, when a woman from a nearby booth was stung by a bee on her hand. Her confusion and the fear on her face told me something was seriously wrong. Concerned, I approached her to see if my wife Linda and I could help. She immediately showed me her swollen hand and told us about her allergies. She didn't have her bee sting kit with her.

This woman was scared! I told her about the energies of Shamballa and asked for her hand. At this point, I think I could have told her anything, because I soon had her hand in mine. As her fear eased, so did the swelling in her hand and the confusion in her face turned to astonishment and tears.

After receiving a tearful thank you from the woman, Linda and I finished our packing and went home, knowing in our hearts that we were able to help someone. Looking back, I owe a lot to that woman. In her confusion, all I saw was someone in need, and in that need I was able to overcome my fears of inadequacy and ridicule to stand in my own power and trust in myself to help her overcome her troubles. At this point, I thought this was the end of the story, but the powers that be had more in mind!

To put things in perspective, I live in Hampden, Maine. Machias is about 120 miles away, and Elsworth is about 60 miles. So to encounter the people in this story would not be an everyday occurrence. Eight months later Linda and I went to Elsworth to attend a concert. In line behind me was a familiar face that I couldn't quite place, and I seemed familiar to her also. Later, during intermission, we met once again, but this time she said, "You're the man—bee sting!" She said that she had told everyone about the bee sting incident, but that not many had believed her. I asked how she was feeling now, and with that I went on my way, thinking it was nice to see her again. However, what little do I know?

Linda and I were asked to cater a pig roast for a hunting club, sponsored at the house of a cardiac doctor with whom Linda worked. During the day the doctor's daughter, who was a friend of our son's, hurt her ankle. We went off to where it was quiet and I treated her with Shamballa energy. A man came in with his dog and asked if he could sit in. He was a dentist and was interested in energy work. Later I went back to cooking, and soon this team of man and dog came over to keep me company. I was waiting for the moment when he would start telling me his problems. It wasn't long! He asked if the Shamballa energies could help with depression. He said that he was trying to get through a terribly bitter divorce from a woman who was a royal__(etc.), and that his best therapy at the moment was his dog.

The topic changed to our making jewelry, and he asked if we ever ran into his wife. A picture of the bee sting woman came to mind, but I let things run their course. This man dumped his bitterness about his ex-wife, and how each time they met to arrange whatever finances needed working out, they ended up fighting, although the last time they had met he had noticed a change in her. He said, "She was actually nice" and they could talk amicably!

After hearing his story, I asked if his ex-wife had bee allergies and made a certain type of jewelry. This woman was one in the same! Evidently, there was more healing going on that I wasn't aware of! I gave him a book to read and my phone number, in case he had any questions or if I could help in any way.

A month and a half passed, and I received a call from this man, just to talk. He had questions about NPMDT, Reiki and energy, which I answered to the best of my knowledge. He also asked for someone in his area who could give him a session. With permission, I sent a distant session and gave him a contact of a trusted Reiki Master (who has now completed Basic NPMDT Master training) and left it at that.

The next year, due to the rainy weather and economic fears, the festival was slow, so we all had time to socialize and barter with each other. I observed the bee sting lady, and I saw a difference in how she treated customers. She seemed more personable than the previous year.

We had time to talk, and I briefly mentioned meeting her ex-husband and his dog. She told me that, once the swelling went down, her hand went back to normal. We found out that as kids we grew up about six miles from each other in Massachusetts. On our way home, Linda gave me a gift from the woman, not to be opened until we were on the road home. In her appreciation and love she gave me a rose quartz wand. Who would have thought that by the simple act of helping, where the ripples of our acts will go. The Machias Blueberry Festival and Lawrence Massachusetts have more in common with Reiki, the Shamballa energies and myself. It seems to be a common thread in my awakening.

One evening we got a call from S.B. of Dover, NH, who had received a pair of our earrings from a friend of hers. The friend had purchased them the previous year at the Machias Festival, but unfortunately she had lost our information card. This year she received another pair and immediately inquired about our wholesale policies. As our relationship grew, she spoke about Reiki and then Shamballa. It seems that when we were kids we also lived within six miles of each other, in Lawrence. As far as I'm concerned, Sue awakened my "Grail Codes", for which I send her many loving thanks. Sue also activated me to Basic Master, which redirected my family's lives as well as my own. It's hard to understand how synchronicities work the way they do. The old saying "God works in mysterious ways" is the truest statement that I've ever heard. So trust in the allowing and enjoy riding the flow.

MASTER TEACHER OF MYSELF

Maurice A. Richard, Jr. (Rochester, NH, USA)

Dear brothers and sisters, the I Am That I Am beckons to all, a time to start living in the now and remember past times of loves and lives that we have touched. Letting the ego go frees us to be who we really are and what reality we have created freely. It is no little task to submit how we have been affected by the freeing power of New Paradigm MDT, the energies of Shamballa. I see a new being that I have created, that has the capability of seeing into the future, now. I see a being capable of bringing his life force to bear against the daily fear of high energy costs. No matter what it costs, I will be able to manifest income to fulfill the need as I need it. There are times when I just have to sit and meditate to bring myself to the frontal attack that I am faced with daily, for there is no good news. Hundreds of thousands of people are presently ascending at this moment as I write this. They have chosen this time to manifest All-That-Is good in mankind.

I rejoice in their ascension. Simplistically, there is no need to submit to anything or anyone, to submit to any power or Monad, for to do this would be folly. FREEDOM is the issue. When you give your freedom away to anything or anyone, you are NO LONGER FREE. That is a simple fact, written in simple English. It is easy to understand. You do not need to be a theologian or religious nut to understand this. It is as it is. What John has taught me through NPMDT is that I was always free. All I had to do was recognize that reality, and I created that moment in my life forever, to be indelibly inscribed in the Akashic record for all eternity. I do simply declare that I am free and I have the power to show others how to be free forever. I have the right to pass on to all who wish to be free, the reality to be free as well. I have the ability to show others how to use Source and its energy. I have the ability to help those who want to heal themselves; I am the conduit that allows Source to flow through my entity, and I allow it to do all that the other person wants in respect to healing. I Am not a healer, but I am part of the one called Source, that allows healing to take place. I Am one that is free, and I will always be free. I declare my freedom for all to see, in love.

ROSALIE'S MINISTRY
Rosalie Spindler (USA)

Rosalie was 69 when her daughter introduced her to the energies of Shamballa. She had no idea what this "energy work" was about, but her daughter, Diane, was so enthusiastic about it, she was open to learning. Little did she know at the time it would not only change her life, but the lives of people she loved.

Following her first two activations, Rosalie noticed her hands would get warm when she brought in the Shamballa energy with the thought "Shamballa on." Her hands were never warm, even in the summer, so she knew something was happening. Also, Rosalie suffered from pancreatitis, and her doctors were surprised she was doing as well as she was. They had predicted her demise a few years ago because that was how this disease usually went. After being attuned to the four levels available at the time, Rosalie started using this energy on herself to take the pain in her stomach away. It worked every time. Over ten years later, she was still beating the odds.

But Rosalie's favorite use of the energy was for long distance healing. She was not well and spent a lot of time sitting quietly at home. She did not get out much. She envisioned her "Shamballa folks sitting on a fence," waiting to help her send healing energy out to anyone she heard about that needed it. This was her way to do some good in the world. At first her list was fairly short, but as people heard about her mission, they would ask her to include them in her ministries. Miraculously, many people she attended to improved.

One day her older sister called her with terrible news. Her husband was in the hospital and dying. The doctors had suggested that the family be called in to say good-bye. He had cancer, and they did not expect him to live much longer. When she called, Rosalie offered to send him Shamballa energy, and her sister was so desperate that she gratefully accepted the offer. Within minutes of Rosalie calling on her "people on the fence," Danny started to improve. He lived another six years, sometimes feeling well enough to go back to work for periods at a time. Whenever he would become ill again, Rosalie would get a call asking her to send energy, and each time he seemed to recoup quickly. He recently died in his mid-eighties, having outlived the doctors' predictions by many years.

Up until her own transition in 2011, Rosalie had a long list of people she sent daily the energies of Shamballa. People had heard about her from friends of friends and asked for her blessings. The thing that continued to surprise her was that people seemed to improve after she brought in the "fence people." This work brought new meaning to her life, and she was eternally grateful to have been taught it so many years ago.

IN TIME

Esther Hoffmann (Groningen, The Netherlands)
Chapter of the travelblog "Een Spirituele Reis Door China"

There was a time that I lived only with Spirit and didn't understand who and where I was. I kept my world safe and didn't move an inch. Of course this had consequences, as I didn't develop as a person in the world called Planet Earth. Since NPMDT entered my life, I opened up and let the outer world come in and the inner world come out. It took quite some years to harmonize and bring balance to the inner world with the outer world. But to keep my inner world as pure as I could the NPMDT philosophy and teachings helped me a lot, while my I Am Presence was my guidance for the outer world.

In the year 2011 I went on a trip to China with Hari Baba. For that trip I kept a travelblog called "A Spiritual Journey across China". I wrote about the meditations and my little adventures with my I Am. Up until today I'm connected and communicating with my I Am Presence because as a result the outer world seems to be merged with the inner world—as above, so below, as within, so without.

So I invite you to join me at the beginning of my trip, catching a plane and communicating with my I Am Presence, which is the 3rd blogpage called "In Time" from my 2011 travelblog:

My I Am Presence is always present and takes good care of me. My I Am Presence takes care that I don't get into trouble. It can make time stand still (!). Or rather, it can make people, things or situations slow down my hurried pace and, hence, seem to prolong time (!). Ultimately, it takes care that the synchronicity in my world works! It makes me grateful and reminds me that life is meaningful and purposeful.

Actually for today, I just had not enough time to arrange my last "little things," going to the groceries, upgrading my travel insurance, drawing extra money from the ATM, checking whether there was enough money on my public travel card, sewing my button on my jacket, collecting the garbage and dropping it off, closing my suitcase with the key which was still missing....

In short, for all this I had only two hours left. Who in their crazy mind would have to arrange so much so shortly before departure? So I took a half-hour delay into account, and reckoned I could be on time at the 'gate' for my 17 o'clock flight to Munich. That's how I thought.

Although people in the grocery shop and at the ATM slowed my pace ("hurry up, hurry up!"), and even though I still had to do so many things, time seemed to feel no longer like I would normally experience. It was strange to be on time for the bus that just drove up, while I knew I normally couldn't catch it because I was really too late. It was strange to sit fifteen minutes early in a relatively empty train while I'm used to catching the train at the last minute. And it was even stranger what happened next at Schiphol Airport Amsterdam.

Because I was early in time, 3 hours before departure-time, I sauntered over to the check-in desk for that one suitcase I was carrying. There were hardly any early fellow travellers, so it quickly was my turn. When the ground stewardess checked my information, she was shocked because I was right on time for my next new early flight; I hadn't had a minute to lose. My 17 o'clock flight was cancelled and I had to take the next flight, which luckily had a delay of one hour due to the fog in Munich. I could just get aboard if I now passed Security.

Security? I only saw thick rows of people up to 15 meters long, a place packed full of people. What security? With the help of the ground stewardess I could avoid the long queue. And so I took the earlier flight of 13 o'clock with a delay of one hour to Munich.

And that's how my I Am Presence had ensured that I came across EXACTLY on time in China.

If I could not have taken this flight, e.g. because I took the next train, I would have missed my flight to Beijing, and I would have had to leave a day later.

And now because of my communication with my I AM Presence I was there where I wanted to be: in China!"

[You can read the complete travelblog in Dutch at http://een-spirituele-reis-door-china.reismee.nl/reisverhalen/]

WHAT SHAMBALLA MEANS TO ME

Cyndi Swenson (Rutland, MA, USA)

This website describes what Shamballa always was to me: http://www.newshamballa.com/tonyknight1.html. Shamballa was a land I once knew and remembered when I heard the name Shamballa. In *Kung fu*, with Kwai Chang Caine, it was a place the Tibetan monks could go to. I saw it when I started using the energy. The people had light bodies when I saw them, and there was peace & love.

I saw C.M. giving someone energy work, and I asked what it was. Immediately I wanted these teachings and activations. The first class she did she attuned me with the symbols. I saw many downloads of symbols, as in *The Matrix* movie, the black screen with the lime green symbols, just falling like hard rain. My eyes fluttered, my mind tried to see each symbol. I was opened once again to what I loved and missed. Everyone always talked about Reiki, but I did not like the sound of Reiki. I love the Shamballa energy; it reminds me of home. The higher the energy got the better. I know I vibrate at a higher level than most, and I have a hard time with the lower energies. I thank

Baba for bringing it in to the US, and Phyllis and Mark for teaching it. Dream the dream, Freedom!

LET THERE BE LIFE

Millie Knox (Mississippi, USA)

One day while I was sitting in the sanctuary at the back of my house in Alexandria, I am interrupted by a phone call from my hairdresser. She said, "Millie, you must come to help me, I am in PICU at Fairfax Hospital, and my daughter, my baby, is in a coma and the doctors have given up on her. She was hit by a car, and they induced a coma to allow her to heal, but she has not come out of it, and the doctors say she probably won't. I know you are a Sufi of sorts and a holy one for sure. Please come, I don't know what else to do."

I left immediately for the hospital, and arrived a short time later. I magically found a place to park close to an entrance, and made my way into the hospital. I followed the signs to PICU, and made good time getting there. I was dressed in my long black skirt, a fluffy white blouse, and sandals. I went down the hallway drawn to the far corner of the building. I didn't know the name to look for but I slowly walked past each room sensing where I am supposed to be. After one complete round in PICU, I decided to send healing to everyone there. I asked permission from each I am Presence, I sent Mahatma Energy to all for about ten minutes.

My hairdresser came running down the hall shouting my name. She took my arm and led me back to her daughter's room. There were two doctors and a nurse in the room, but my hairdresser shooed them out saying, "My healer is here. You had your chance. Now I want you to leave." The doctors were extremely offended, but they left grumbling.

I sat in a chair next to the bed and connected with the child. I saw her standing in a sphere of light, and spoke to her, "Hello there, your mother misses you very much, and she would like you to follow me back to her."

When I came back to the room, the child was wide awake and squeezing my arm. I kissed her on the wound bandaged at her head, and she smiled and said, "Hello again, thank you." Just then, four doctors came rushing into the room. I heard the word miracle several times, but managed to slip out of the room unnoticed. The child is well now and back in school with no lasting effects except a slight limp. I am grateful for John and the experiences in the trainings with him. I continue to shine as bright as I can, everywhere I can, and do what I can for those who come to me.

MY 13D WORKSHOP WAS INCREDIBLE.
Mary Beth Curry (Roseville, MN, USA)

I feel immense joy, gratitude, hopefulness, and a great need for a nap or two after such a dynamic and high frequency experience with the 20 students in my workshop. It was truly phenomenal. I could feel the support of our entire Holland class, Francis, my teacher, and you [Phyllis] and Susan. And, of course, John was right beside me as I did the activations. I could feel/see him many times. And the Masters were truly guiding me. I changed things/the schedule many times as we went along. It flowed effortlessly and perfectly according to the way I felt and comments of the students, which verified they felt the same way.

I felt a "click" or "ka-chink" early on in this class, like my whole being clicked into a slot or position in a perfect fit, and everything was fun, easy, relaxed, and really flowing. It just was/is. No big deal. And the class was a joy. I felt, "these are my people", and I felt great gratitude to be able to work with them and to be a part of the impact we're all having on life in these times. And it's so beautiful to watch their unfolding in the class, before it, after it, etc. I also invited in anyone in the "collective" on a soul level who wanted to receive the workshop/activations to join us. I also invited in Mother Earth. So what happened was much, much bigger than just these 20 people. And we felt it and saw it sometimes. It was beautiful and amazing work. And the students are changed people after experiencing it. Amazing what can happen when you become an instrument for the Divine! One of them said to me: "This is really beautiful. You are teaching unconditional love."

I feel physically weary right now but also very wonderful and peaceful. This is such glorious work!

WHY I TOOK 13D A SECOND TIME

Francis van Dusseldorp (Wageningen, The Netherlands)

Dear friends, some of us humans find the course a bit expensive, and of course it is a lot of money, which I could use for a summer vacation for example. Last November I did the course for the second time. Not that I didn't pass the test the first time, I already had a wonderful certificate and had already started giving the basic workshops. At first, when I signed up for this class, I was a bit embarrassed by myself and found it a little bit stupid to do the same training twice. But as I had learned to follow my guidance, even if I didn't fully understand the point, I arranged my life to attend this class.

During the workshop it became clear to me that I was there to learn, and most of all accept, channeling my own I Am Presence. And I remembered that that was indeed my objective in attending the first 13D teacher class one and a half years ago. This second class facilitated for me a huge overcoming of mistrust towards my own I Am. Now I know my I Am has the same agenda as me: namely BEING FREE and SELF-LOVE. This makes it so much easier for me to live my life and do my things and walk my path. Not that I live a hallelujah life every day; it is more about accepting myself with love and taking my steps gently, to stand more and more in my own power. I thank my teacher, Hari Baba, for it with all my heart.

Since then I have given a 13D Healer workshop, and I immediately felt the difference. My I Am came through frequently in the channeling of meditations, and the connection with the I Am's of the students was felt more direct. Most of all, I was able to share and show what NPMDT aims, a growing/expanding conscious connection with your own I Am. It did feel rather strange at first to channel my own I Am. I can recommend it to every teacher to give it a try, if you are not already doing it in a workshop. Now I can hear you think, "Everybody does channel already his/her I Am! and certainly a NPMDT teacher!" This is true, as we know, but we are still channeling a lot of the multi-dimensional masters, aren't we. At least I was and still am. We do this because we think we need them, and that we cannot do the required things/meditations/clearings without them. Sure, their assistance is very helpful and welcome, BUT it is we who are in command of our own power. So, channeling consciously, out loud, your own I Am IS, at that moment, standing in your own power, even regardless of the outcome! And from that point on we can call in the assistance of ANYONE we would like. Now, isn't that great!

Tomorrow I start another 13D workshop, and this one is a direct flow from the last one. A student of mine who had finished the 13D last December wanted to continue her empowering process. Her enthusiasm convinced friends of hers to do the same course. So she will attend the 13D for the second time. I, her teacher, had done the 13D Teacher twice and had clearly explained that, in fact, none of the NPMDT workshops are ever the same, that it is always a next step into your own mastery. She just follows her own flow, and I thank her for it.

THE PURPOSE OF NPMDT [using the energies of Shamballa]
Kathleen Daykin (The Netherlands)

I have been spending a lot of time talking with Germain and the Lords and Ladies of Shamballa about NPMDT. One of my questions to Germain was what his actual job is regarding NPMDT, his job description, if you like. I would like to share the answer with you.

Germain's job is to gently and lovingly usher in the energies of Shamballa and to support the sharing or spreading of the energies to as many people as possible, as quickly as possible. This is the first part of his job.

The second part is to support and facilitate the forming, through the first part, of a web of love/light (a grid or a network) that also then forms a sanctuary for all those grounding in this energy.

It deeply moved me when I heard the word *sanctuary* come through. Then I thought, NPMDT Sanctuary, with a bit of a smile. But I quickly heard a *no*. It is not a NPMDT sanctuary, but goes far beyond that. NPMDT is a means to spread the energies of love and light, and also a means for us to connect with each other and bundle our intentions. But this web of light goes further beyond NPMDT, even if it is initiated or facilitated by it.

What was shown me is that every single one of us is a crucial part of this NPMDT project and needed for the project to come together. Each one has their own role to play. As Germain has his role and Hari Baba has his role, so does each one of us. The role of each one also needs to be respected and honored by all. If we don't form it together then it won't get formed; it's as simple as that. Germain cannot do this without us. This last may be pretty obvious, as we are the ones who ground into 3D, but I am saying it anyway.

As some of you may know, I am one of the group of people working for the organizations of NPMDT. My job is such that most queries, comments, requests, and criticisms [at least in Europe] pass to me first. So I have a pretty good view of how things are developing in the NPMDT family. I think that it is pretty fair to say that regarding the first part of Germain's task, we are doing pretty well. Regarding the second part, I would say we have quite a way to go before that is manifested and grounded. Some of us are connecting with others in various ways, but a very large portion of those grounding the energies of Shamballa are kind of single candles burning on lonely islands.

The image that came to mind when I felt the word *sanctuary* was of a sailing ship limping into a small sheltered harbor: a place to do repairs after stormy seas, a place to get fresh food and water, medicines if needed, new cargo to take elsewhere, and where new workers can be hired to go along. What kind of reception does the ship get when it sails into the harbor?

When we have been activated to these energies of Shamballa, a lot of stuff gets activated and cleared, and we are expanding our consciousness. The old system of levels 1 through 4 was like driving in first gear. Then in the Basic workshops we shifted up to 2nd or 3rd gear, and in the 13D moved into warp drive. As everybody knows, the more light the more dirt you can see, and the growth of consciousness does not stop at the end of the workshop. Many people are then working through all kinds of processes that a lot of friends and family no longer understand or support, and it can become very lonely and confusing for a while. And right about then a sanctuary might be very helpful!

I wonder how many people have been glad to hear that there is a NPMDT Yahoo talk group, and hoped to find some kind of sanctuary there? And did they find it? And I wonder what gives a sense of finding a sanctuary, because there are probably quite a number of different needs for that too. I wonder how many people have somewhere to go and share the new understandings and experiences they are undergoing, including sometimes the loss of lifelong friends because of these changes? I wonder how many of us truly feel a sense of connection and support within the NPMDT family? And do we want that? In Love.

FROM FAUN FENDERSON

(New Orleans, LA, USA)

More than any other quality or benefit or insight that I've acquired from my NPMDT relationship (most all of which have been lovingly described by others in this book), I truly feel and appreciate the energetic connection to the NPMDT Family. Knowing that there are others "out there" is extremely comforting and also liberating—they make sharing the love is so easy!

My love to you! Faun

SILENCE, LIGHT, BALANCE AND *LOVE*

Emilia Dragomir—NPMDT Basic Master Workshop (Bucharest, Roumania, 2013)

My name is Emilia Dragomir and for this testimony I use a few words, apparently common. But they are not just words, they are my experience that I lived during the Basic workshop New Paradigm MDT.

About my path until NPMDT: during my childhood, I had some developed senses (hearing and eyesight), and my parents thought about me as a precocious child. In those days nobody spoke about radioestesy, Reiki, Huna, NPMDT.

The years have passed, and I grew up and I had the chance to learn radioestesy, only 3 degrees because my soul did not allow to continue this path and I always follow my soul.

Then I met my Huna teacher and the Huna energies in April 2012: great ... awesome, you find yourself, your soul knows high vibration, you feel loved and caressed by divinity.

Through my curiosity and the desire for evolution, I was determined to continue the search and so I met New Paradigm MDT.

With the same person I crossed this experience can not be described by words ... namely SHAM-BA-LLA, SHAM-BA-LLA, SHAM-BA-LLA. I felt an inner peace, warmth in my soul and inside of my body. Pink and gold, yellow and then Violet Flame, were the colors that accompanied me during this journey. Archangel Michael was present beside me and I felt Him like a shield, He held my hand and we traveled together through the galaxies, up to the Heart of God, without any fear and full of enthusiasm. I knew that I am not alone.

Through New Paradigm MDT energies and Mahatma everyone meets the higher vibrations, and through the Ascended Masters –its own healing, but also the transformation of others.

New Paradigm MDT opened my golden path, my wonderful and magnificent path!

And a completion, October 2014:

Then I encountered attempts, health problems. But I feel Baba and I feel my NPMDT sisters and brothers when they assist me with their love and that makes me strong, I know that I am not alone, and I am grateful for them.

And I feel Mother Earth when She moans of suffering and I know that we are all Her children on this road forever. Shamballa ON!—Emilia

NPMDT and ME

Barbara J. Allen, Child of the Universe

Back in 2000/2001 several of my friends suggested that I look into Reiki; they thought it would interest me. I never looked into it. Then, one day, I heard the word Shamballa. I signed up immediately to learn this modality. What I did not know at the time was that I had just started on the Path Home.

From Levels I-IV all the way to New Paradigm Multi-Dimensional Transformation, I have been along for the ride. I use NPMDT in everything I do.

I started "teaching" as soon as I could. I wanted to spread this shift to everyone, children and adults alike. I found that the Shamballa Energy enhances everything I do—whether it was working with my animals, the gardening I was doing at the time as a way to earn a living, the children in my life, my cooking, everything. I learned to incorporate gems, crystals and herbs into the work, using them alone or in conjunction with the healing aspect of NPMDT. There are no limits as to what you can do with this amazing energy. It is truly Multi-dimensional.

Then, there are the people I met. Finally, to meet so many like minded beings. I recognize them all, from a different time and place? A different lifetime? I don't know, it might just be that I recognize the Love and the Light that we all share.

My first meeting with Hari Das/Hari Baba/John Armitage back in 2001 really confirmed that this was where I was meant to be. I remember driving to the workshop with two friends. The closer we got, the more nervous I got. What had I gotten myself into??? Nine days with 26 people and Baba. OH MY. Well, my friends and I got settled into our shared room and we set out to greet Baba. As soon as he arrived, and I saw that he is "just a man", I calmed down, and the rest is history. I now call Baba a friend, a part of my family.

I do not think a day goes by that I don't call on the energy of NPMDT for one reason or another. I still love "teaching" the work, spreading the Love and the Light as often as I can. I will continue with NPMDT no matter what it is called, and I hope to continue to teach and facilitate healings for as long as I can. This is more than worth sharing—this is worth Living.

In Love, Light, Laughter and Munay

MORE COMMENTS FROM NPMDT WORKSHOPS

I use the 'work' every day, but it is not work. I feel like I walk in wonder even at work much of the time. A.

I have been working with this energy for about six months now. It has made a huge difference in my personal process and self-healing. The classes are great—M.B. is a supportive and passionate teacher. You receive a lot of clearing and healing in the workshops. This is a great experience for anyone who is interested in expanding their consciousness and learning new things about healing. I recommend this to everyone!

In the light, T.E.

I have more breathing room now, thank Goddess. I see what you mean about the differences between this energy and Reiki. I have made a lot of major changes in my life after my NPMDT workshop, far more dramatic than after Reiki. I feel FREE, and I am living my life the way I feel called to live it. I am definitely interested in doing a class so I can teach. J.D.

I feel like a new person and cannot wait to put it all to good use. B.L.

I awoke this morning to the realization that the past 4 days were a life changing experience for me, but only if I keep the lessons and practices in my daily life. Thank you so much for the gift you and all of those you channeled have given me.

Thank you! The energy of Shamballa has changed my practice, and my life. T.C.

I want to thank you for the class. It was a wonderful and powerful and cleansing experience, and the Shamballa energy is really helping me in my personal evolution. M.H.

I was attuned to the Shamballa energy by A.S. a few years ago. I have mostly done healings for myself, friends and family, but am now starting to work with people I have never met! It has been an interesting test for me, and I feel my confidence growing with each healing I facilitate. It is so wonderfully rewarding to do something so easy as to just open up to these amazing energies and have people leave my home feeling so good! E.H.

My recent class (Basic Master Teacher) was, well words cannot describe it. It was just life altering and transformative. I am so very grateful for the energy of Shamballa and what it does for me and can do for others, if they just allow the love to flow. I Am that I Am, the Mahatma in love. Shamballa ON! C.M.

CHAPTER 9

NPMDT COURSES, TEACHERS, CONTACTS

NOW is the time to release all unnecessary programs from the past and to prepare to receive the new energies coming in. We are co-creating here on Earth things beyond our imagination. You are invited to be present in each and every moment, and to enjoy the dance through to the end of time. —Hari Das Baba /John Armitage & Germain

NEW PARADIGM MDT CLASSES AVAILABLE

BASIC MASTER: (2 days/16 hours) We focus on releasing old programming, accepting yourself as a divine creative being, and welcoming the energies of Personal Transformation, of Love and Freedom. No prerequisites. Graduates are encouraged to take 13D Master, which is of a higher frequency. Graduates may also take Basic Teacher. Includes manual and Basic Master certificate.

BASIC MASTER TEACHER: (3 days/24 hours) Available to Basic Master and 13D Master graduates who wish to teach Basic Master. Includes official manual and official Basic Master Teacher certificate.

13 DIMENSIONAL MASTER: (4 days/32 hours) Initiations into the highest and most recent evolutionary energies available to humanity on this planet. Clearings, code activations, DNA clearings and activations. 13 activations into the New Paradigm MDT energies. No prerequisites. Anyone who feels called to can take this course.

13D UPGRADE: (2 days/16 hours) The energies available to us increase constantly and exponentially. This course brings to 13D graduates the latest energies for release and personal growth, as well as more personal activations. Available to 13D graduates, preferably from their own 13D teacher, if he or she has had the Upgrade training from Baba, or from another 13D teacher if necessary.

13 DIMENSIONAL TEACHER TRAINING INTENSIVE: (9 days) This is taught only by Hari Baba himself. It includes the 13 Dimensional NPMDT activations (with a focus on learning to pass them on to others), plus further activations that each receives under the guidance of their own I Am Presence, clearing meditations, and hands-on energy work practice. Much time is spent learning to channel and practicing channeling. The 9-day intensive with Hari Baba is a life-changing experience. Those who qualify at the end (who can channel for around 5 minutes in front of the class) receive a certificate entitling them to teach 13D Master. Some take this course just for the experience and personal growth, and do not want to do the channeling (or get a certificate). Prerequisite: at least one other NPMDT course.

13D TEACHER UPGRADE: (2 days/16 hours) Taught only by Hari Baba, this brings teachers of 13D up to date with the current energies and meditations, so that they may pass these on to their students.

OTHER COURSES FROM THE SCHOOL OF ESOTERIC SCIENCES

(taught by John Armitage/Hari Das Baba)

- **Crystal Sciences**
- **Gem Remedies I-IV**
- **Ascension**
- **Memories of the Soul**
- **Ascending with the New Earth**
- **Journey Into Oneness**
- **Pathway to the Cosmic Heart**
- **[And others to come]**

WEBSITES & TEACHERS

www.new-paradigm-mdt.org

Official website of the School of Esoteric Sciences throughout the world. Information on the school, courses, teachers, the various Associations, Baba's teaching schedule, our projects throughout the world.

www.taliloquay.com

Source of NPMDT CD's, DVD's and White Powder Gold essence in the Americas

John Armitage's websites:

www.johnarmitage.me (some meditations available to listen to here)

www.crystalskulls.johnarmitage.me

Facebook: New Paradigm MDT Founder Group

GLOSSARY

Adam Cadmon light body: (Vywamus channeled through John Armitage) *The crystalline light body, this adam cadmon body of perfection. I will attempt to give you more clarity on what this adam cadmon body is, and how each and every one of you were created. All of you starry beings, starry brothers and sisters, you all came here from other places. You came here at a certain time, of the seeding of the races upon the planet. Before Mother Earth had a solidity about her body, she was fluid, gas and particles. Before that she was a finer, or higher vibrational energy. As the body of Mother Earth became more solid, you needed different bodies through which to experience this reality. Previously, in the times that you may relate to as Lemurian times, you had bodies of light. You communicated through your thoughts, you manifested everything through thought. You meditated the trees into being. You meditated the crystals into being, the seas and the rivers, everything. And then, as the solidification took place more and more and more, your light bodies weren't the vehicles that you needed to experience in this reality, because of the incompatibility of the vibrations. So human bodies were created. Many would think that the creator of the human bodies, Yahweh, is the creator of all things—in fact religious philosophies, both Christian and the others, believe that Yahweh is absolute God. That is not true. Yahweh is the creator of your human bodies. Where does Yahweh live? Even today Yahweh lives in the constellation of Orion. Yahweh was charged by the creators of Mother/*

Father God to create bodies of perfection and harmony, bodies through which people, or beings, could realize in this dimensional reality that they are harmony, balance, love, and the other things that go along with it. So the human bodies were created, and you were also given a body of light, a body of perfection, a body of harmony, love. Through the integration into your body physical of this light body, this adam cadmon body, you become light. Remember the word, "enlighten". You become light!

Akashic Record: History of humanity and Earth that is held electro-magnetically around the planet accessible by higher vibrational humans. Sometimes called the "cosmic mind" or the "collective consciousness", it is said to record every thought, word and action of every human since the beginning of time in this universe.

Andromedans: Extra-terrestrial group from Andromeda who work with others to help humanity and the earth through the ascension process. John/Baba says that the Andromedans are soldier-protectors, and he has worked with them many times.

Antahkarana: Tube of light that runs through the center of a human body, energetically connecting the major chakras.

Apollonius of Tyana: Charismatic teacher and worker of miracles from the first century AD. Sananda has said through J.A. that this was his last human lifetime on earth.

Ascended Master: Usually refers to one who has lived as a human on earth and achieved mastery over Self, being able to travel multi-dimensionally without first having to die. This is achieved by raising one's vibrational rate to the necessary level. Beings from other planetary systems have also ascended and are also a part of the Lords and Ladies of Shamballa, or the Great Brotherhood of Light.

Ashtar: Leader of "the airborn division of the Great White Brotherhood" or Ashtar Command, who are here to help humanity ascend dimensionally, become peaceful, and join the Galactic Brotherhood. Not all "channelings" reputed to come from the Ashtar Command (and circulating wildly on the internet) are actually from there, however. The dark brothers and sisters enjoy confounding and misleading people by pretending to be of the Brotherhood of Light. Always the seeker must be discerning.

Atlantis, Atlantean: Referring to an ancient civilization that existed mostly on a continent in what is now the Atlantic Ocean. A high level civilization powered by crystals and mental skills, it existed for over 100,000 years, finally destroying itself and much of the then-known world in the last of a series of 5 cataclysms, around 12,000 years ago.

Axiatonal Lines: These have nothing to do with your meridians, or your etheric matrix. They are different. They run up and down the body and keep us very firmly connected to Mother Earth.

Brahmin: Hindu priest/holy man; one who knows *Brahman, the unchanging, infinite, immanent, and transcendent reality which is the Divine Ground of all matter, energy, time, space, being and everything beyond in this Universe* (Wikipedia definition).

Chakra: From the Sanskrit "spinning wheel". Energy centers of the human body's electro-magnetic systems; they act as transformers for the life force energy as it descends (vibrationally speaking) from Source to the human body, lowering its frequency so that it is usable by the human body in 3D. They connect the various bodies of the human (physical, etheric, emotional, mental, spiritual). There are seven major chakras along the center of the body, connected by the antahkarana, or tube of light. There are many, many more chakras throughout the body; wherever the electro-magnetic lines of energy of the etheric body/meridians cross is a chakra. These are the points that acupuncture and acupressure practitioners stimulate in order to bring the body back into balance.

Channeling: Communication with higher dimensional beings by means of the antahkarana or "channel" of light that runs through the human body. Word was coined by Ramtha in the 1980's to describe the way in which he, as an entity from 35,000 years ago, came into and spoke through a woman from Washington, USA. That method is known as "trance" channeling, in which the entity communicating fully takes over the physical body of the channeler. Baba/John Armitage uses a different form, in which the channeler never gives away the body, but is present and can hear and interact with the entity communicating. Higher-level entities must lower their vibrations in order to come through a human, so it makes sense that humans of the highest vibrations channel the highest vibrational beings. There are many entities from the lower 4th dimension who like to come through lower vibrational channelers; it is up to the listener to beware of the content and vibrational level of the channeled message. Most channelers are from 5-50% or so accurate in their rendition of the message. Germain has declared Baba to be 85% accurate or higher, a very high percentage. Trance channelers transmit their messages exactly as they are given; however one must be certain of the integrity of the entity sending the message. All channelings are not the same, or of the same integrity.

Chohan: "Chief", here meaning head or director in charge of the energies of one of the Rays of Creation. The Chohans of the Rays are high vibrational beings of great light and wisdom, who oversee our development here on earth through these energies. See *Rays.*

Das: Shortened form of Haridas, "Servant of God", name given John Armitage by his guru in India.

Deva: Etheric being or energy that holds the energy pattern of a place or plant species, etc. Some devas serve as "guardians" of high-energy places on the earth.

Djwhal Khul: Ascended master who, while living as a monk in Tibet in the early 1900's was "channeled" by Alice Bailey to create volumes of esoteric teachings. He is Chohan (Lord) of the Second Ray, and a great teacher.

Dr. Usui: Japanese Buddhist monk who discovered healing symbols in Sanskrit writings in the early 1900's and used them, along with a few other Japanese symbols, to create a healing system he called "Reiki", meaning "life force" in Japanese.

Etheric: Being of a higher vibrational frequency than is visible with normal human eyesight (higher than 3rd dimension).

El Morya: Ascended Master and Chohan (Lord) of the First Ray (of God's Will).

Gaia: One of the names for planet Earth, the Goddess Gaia, who is a sentient being.

Galaxiatonal Lines: At one time we knew we had axiatonal lines, but didn't understand that we also have galaxiatonal lines, which keep us in touch with the galactic energies in a balanced and easy way.

Germain: Often referred to as St. Germain, an Ascended Master and very great and loving being of Light who has dedicated his very great light and wisdom to the development and ascension of humanity on earth. He is in charge of ushering in the New Golden Age on earth at this time. Among his many incarnations are Pharaoh Akhenaton, the Jewish prophet Samuel, Joseph the father of Jesus, the magician Merlin, Columbus (as a walk-in), and Francis Tudor (illegitimate son of Queen Elizabeth I of England). In this last life he lived on earth under many names over a period of around 400 years, continually staging his own death to come back as another. These personalities included Sir Francis Bacon and Prince Rakoczy. During this time he was responsible for the writings of Christopher Marlowe, William Shakespeare, Edmund Spenser, Montaigne, Robert Burton, Cervantes, the King James Bible, and others. His goal during this very long lifetime was to bring the concept of Freedom to human societies. He attempted to teach the noble classes, especially in France, the error of their ways, to prevent a bloodbath during the French revolution that he knew was coming; as he says in the moving essay on "Gifts" included in this book, he failed in that. This Freedom was also his goal in nurturing what became the United States of America. He brings New Paradigm Multi-Dimensional Transformation to us as well, to teach us of our own divinity, in Freedom and Love without conditions.

Haridas: "Servant of God", name given to John Armitage by his guru when he studied in India to become a Brahmin. Some of John's other lifetimes include Luke, friend and disciple of Jesus during his Palestinian ministry; Pharaoh Akhenaten's High Priest; and Washitaka, assistant to Wotana, the medicine man who led the Anasazi of southwest North America in their ascension around 1300. As he states in the Preface, "I was with Shah Jehan at Agra, Francis at Assisi, Kuthumi in Kashmir, Djwhal Khul in Tibet" and others. He is an aspect of Melchizedek and has been gradually integrating higher and higher aspects of himself during this lifetime. He is founder of New Paradigm Multi-Dimensional Transformation, using the energies of Shamballa.

Hari Baba: "Master", name given John fairly recently by Germain.

Hari Das Baba: Name John Armitage prefers to go by now.

Insectoid: One of the three body-types of sentient beings in this creation, the others being humanoid and reptilian or reptoid.

Joseph of Arimathea: Brother of Mary, Uncle of Jesus during his Palestinian lifetime. He was a trader who visited Britain for tin, and he took Jesus and Luke, as teenagers, to study there with the Druids. He was a high ranking Essene who helped to direct and carry out the greater Plan involved in Jesus' ministry and crucifixion.

Kanji: System of Japanese writing using original Chinese pictograms.

Kumara: High vibrational level family of beings who are here from Creator, via the planet Venus, to help humanity and the earth to ascend dimensionally. Sanat Kumara is the planetary Logos, or "soul" of planet earth. Sananda/Jesus is another Kumara. Esoteric literature lists seven Kumaras, or "Lords of the Flame" who in great love offered to guard and guide Earth humans in their spiritual evolution. They are listed as Sanatka (1st Ray, Blue Flame, Will of God), Sa Ananda (2nd Ray, Yellow Flame, Wisdom of God—whose Palestinian Ministry on Earth under the name of Jesus is well-remembered), Sa Na Tana (3rd Ray, Pink Flame, Love of God), Sujata (4th Ray, White Flame, Purity of God), Kapila (5th Ray, Green Flame, Science of God), Sa Na Kumara (6th Ray, Purple-Gold-Ruby Flame, Peace of God), and Sanat Kumara (7th Ray, Violet Flame, Freedom of God—our Planetary Logos).

Kuthumi: Ascended master, one of whose earthly lifetimes was as St. Francis of Assisi.

Lao Tzu: Author of the *Tao te Ching*, "The Way and Its Power", in the 6th century BC.

Lemuria: Very ancient civilization, pre-dating and later co-existing with early Atlantis.

Maitreya: Master name of the Buddha, who overlighted Sananda/ Jesus during his Palestinian ministry.

Melchizedek: Consciousness of the Great Central Sun, director of this Cosmic Day in this Universe. The I Am Presence, or Monad, of John Armitage.

Merkaba or Merkabah: from Egyptian MER or light, KA or life force, and BA or individual personality; also Hebrew "chariot". Vehicle created by consciousness in order to travel upper dimensions; created esoterically by high vibrational initiates. A sacred geometric light field around the body. Baba tells us that Merkaba is an *energy, it is* not the geometric shapes around your body, and these are not the light body. The geometric shapes around your body change as you accelerate your consciousness. They are not the same for everybody.

Namaste: Literally, in Sanskrit, "The Divinity in me (the God in me) bows to (salutes) the Divinity in you."

Ramtha: Being who lived around 35,000 years ago, during the break-up of Lemuria, and became a great conqueror; he then conquered himself, and ascended. He is full-body, or trance, channeled by J.Z. Knight who lives near Seattle, WA, USA. He coined the word "channeling" in the 1980's to describe how he was able to speak to people through her.

Rays: The seven Rays are the seven basic kinds of energies from which this universe is created, and that are available to us on earth. Each has six levels: spiritual, soul, personality, emotional, mental, and physical. Each also has a being or *chohan* that is in charge of that Ray energy on earth. [see *Violet Ray*] Humans come into incarnation influenced by a certain ray on each of the above levels. As one heightens vibration, the next level and it's Ray take over in that person's life. In the 1970's earth was granted 5 new Rays to help with the ascension of earth (and humanity) into the 4th and 5th dimensions (possibly higher). Rays 8-12 are composed of the first seven rays plus the white light of Source, making them luminous.

Reptoid or Reptillian: one of the three body types of sentient beings in this creation, the others being humanoid and insectoid.

Sadhus: Hindu term for ascetics, or practitioners of yoga (Yogi); the "wandering holy men of India".

Sananda: Ascended Master name of Jesus.

Sanat Kumara: Planetary Logos, or "soul" of planet earth (the goddess Gaia). Vywamus is an even higher vibrational aspect.

Sanskrit (Ancient): An historical Indo-Aryan language, Vedic Sanskrit dates back to at least 1500 BCE. Sanskrit is still used liturgically in Hinduism and Buddhism. It has always been considered a sacred "language of the gods" and the surviving large body of literature in Sanskrit dating back to ancient times includes poetry, drama, scientific and philosophical discourses, and religious texts.

Shah Jehan/Jahan: (b.1592, ruled 1627-58) Known as "the Master Builder" and architect of the Taj Mahal; 5th of the 6 rulers of the Mughal Empire, great dynasty of northern India. One of the earth lifetimes of Master Kuthumi (another was St. Francis).

Upstairs Department or Upstairs Crew: John's name for his multi-dimensional friends and helpers.

Violet Ray: Master Germain is chohan of the seventh or Violet Ray [see *Rays*] of Transmutation, often referred to as the Violet Flame which transmutes base or lower vibrations into higher ones. One of Germain's aspects (Merlin) calls this the "true alchemy". This Violet Ray is the Gateway to the New Age.

Vywamus: An incredibly loving energy who says we can consider him a cosmic aspect of Sanat Kumara, who is the soul aspect of Lady Gaia, our planet earth. When I call on him, immediately I feel surrounded and permeated by a beautiful powerful yet gentle love and acceptance. He is especially known for helping to ground the Mahatma energy of love without conditions onto earth, and for helping people to open their channel, or antahkarana, in order to communicate with other dimensions.

Wotanna: Medicine man of the Anasazi just before and during their ascension around 1300 AD; John Armitage/Hari Baba, then Washitaka, was his apprentice and agreed to stay behind to help those who were not able to make the ascension.

Printed in Great Britain
by Amazon